Tregaron
CMS L71, S9, S10
CMS L71, S6
CMS S9, S10
611
Pumpsaint
LLANWRDA
LLANDOVERY
760
750
Llangadog
LLANDEILO
SWT 16, 36
Llandebie
SWT 124
301
612
SWT 120, 130
AMMANFORD
SWT 18, 18A, 121, 122, 135
Brynamman
SWT 121
SWT 18, 18A, 121
601
GWAUN-CAE-GURWEN
SWT 18, 18A, 122
Ystradgynlais
Ystalyfera
Pontardawe
Alltwen
608
SWT 122
Clydach
SWT 3
SWT 22 6
UWS 101
Pontarddulais
SWT 69
Llanwrtyd Wells
Llangammarch Wells
Cilmery
Builth Road
Builth Wells
Newbridge
738
X 71
CG
Llandrindod Wells
CMS S23
Sennybridge
SWT 28
Trallong
Coryton
729
736
BISHOP'S MEADOW
BRECON
Libanus
Storey Arms
CMS X71
RW170
Onllwyn
Banwen
607
Glynneath
604
602
Rhigos (Trading Estate)
603
Rhigos
Cwmgwrach
Hirwaun
ABERDARE
605
RW172
RW171, 175
UWS 114
SWT 114
RW175
SWT17
UWS 31
Glyncorrwg
Blaenrhondda
MERTHYR TYDFIL
RW178
RTC100
Troedyrhiw
Merthyr Vale
Bedlinog
Pant
Dowlais
RW141
RW147
Rhymney Bridge
RW163
Rhymney
Pontlottyn
Fochriw
Tir Phil
Deri
BARGOED
Sirhowy
Tredegar
Trefil
RW 148
504
513
505
RW151
RW145
Beaufort
Ebbw Vale
Garn Lydan
RW 130
Brynmawr
Nantyglo
Blaina
RW127
Six Bells
RW122
RW121
Llyswen
Bronllys
Talgarth
730
739
Glasbury
Llowes
Clyro
Hay-on-Wye
Whitney
Willersley
Eardisley
Brilley
MR440
MR449
RW 39
Dorstone
Peterchurch
Vowchurch
Llangorse
733
Talybont
732
Bwlch
Crickhowell
Capel-y-ffin
RW111
Coed Dias
Pontrilas
RW150
Pandy
RW65
ABERGAVENNY
Llandewi Rhydderch
RW45
Gilwern
RW129
RW133
Govilon
Llanfoist
RW112
Clydach
RW 110
Pwll-du
RW 143
Blaenavon
RW143
Forge Side
704
715
716
717
718
737
Varteg
Cwmavon
British
707
708
Abersychan
Pentwyn
742
Pontnewynydd
701
702
703
712
PONTYPOOL
705
735
Penpergwm
Herbert Arms
RW 117 & 164
RW124
RW164
Glascoed
Usk
RW122, 143
CWMBRAN

GLORY DAYS

Western Welsh

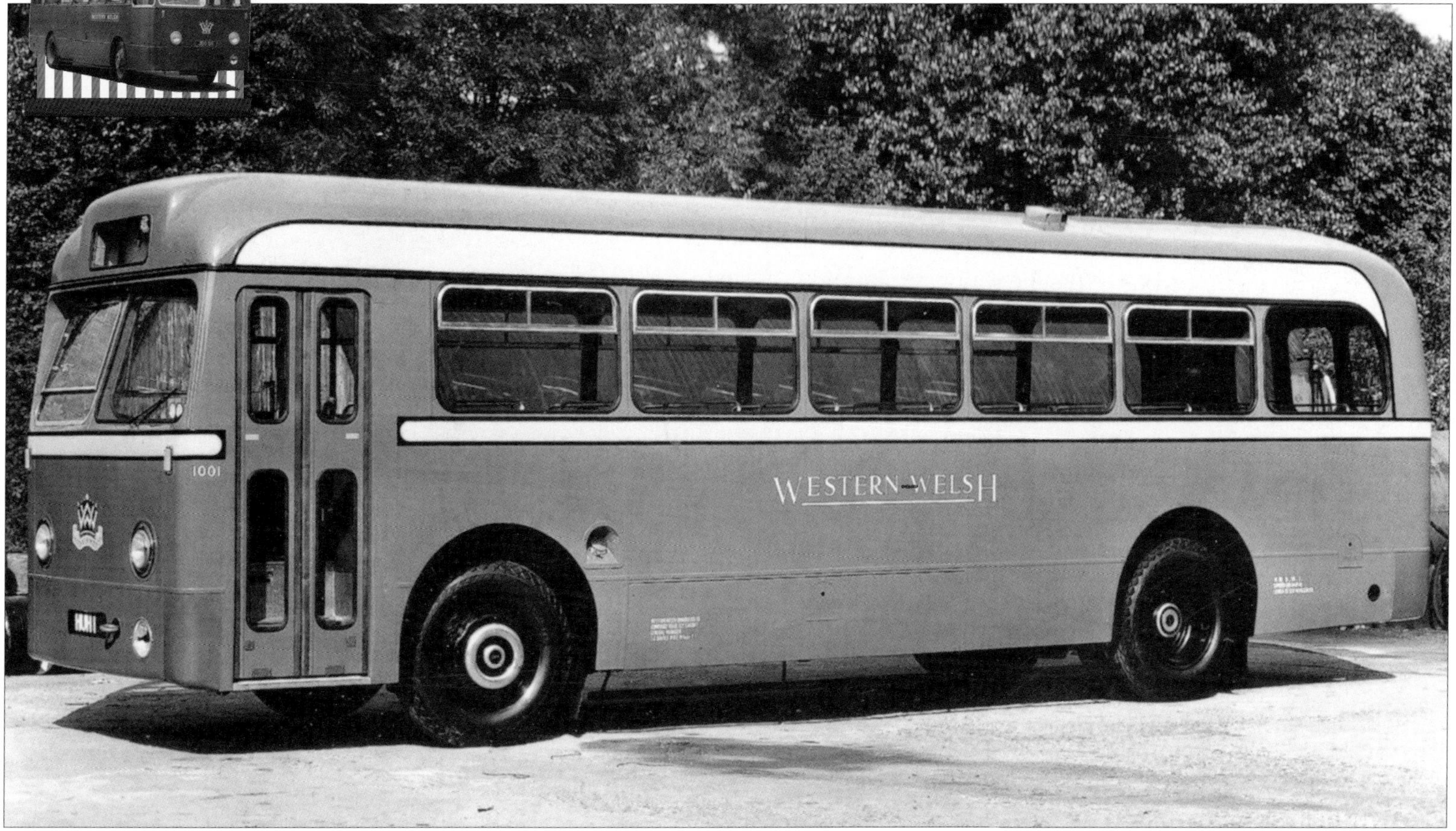

Roger Davies, Chris Taylor and Viv Corbin

Front cover:
A type forever associated with Western Welsh (and constituting the largest fleet of similar-looking double-deck buses ever owned) was the semi-lowbridge Weymann-bodied Atlantean. No 340 of 1962 makes its way through typical scenery at Vale Terrace, Lower Tredegar, nearing the end of its 23-mile run from Newport via Risca, Ynysddu and Blackwood. Despite early problems these buses gave full service lives and more, this one lasting until 1978. *Arnold Richardson / Photobus*

Back cover:
Crossing the River Teifi at the popular beauty spot of Cenarth Falls is 1966 Tiger Cub/ Marshall 1376. It is on service 404 linking Carmarthen with Cardigan, a bit of an epic. Along with Newcastle Emlyn depot, both route and bus would pass to Crosville shortly after this picture was taken in March 1972. *Kenneth Evans*

Contents

Endpapers:
Map of the WW area.
It cost 6d (2½p). *Viv Corbin collection*

Previous page:
The epitome of Western Welsh. The company's first Tiger Cub, Weymann-bodied 1001 of 1953, shows off the fully lined-out livery and the distinctive chunky but attractive fleet numbers. *Viv Corbin collection*

First published 2007

ISBN (10) 0 7110 3217 3
ISBN (13) 978 0 7110 3217 0

Published by Ian Allan Publishing

an imprint of Ian Allan Publishing Ltd, Hersham, Surrey KT12 4RG

Printed in England by Ian Allan Printing Ltd, Hersham, Surrey KT12 4RG

Code: 0711/B

Visit the Ian Allan Publishing website at www.ianallanpublishing.com

The nicely balanced lines of the Northern Counties-bodied Renown are clearly shown in this shot. No 713, the first of 28, was the only one registered in 1964, having been displayed, in true Western Welsh tradition, at that year's Commercial Motor Show. It also differed from the rest in having a straight waistrail over the windscreen, all the rest having this slightly raised, presumably to improve vision. Maybe it was the low centre of gravity, but these were lovely buses to drive. Happily, 713 is now preserved.
Arnold Richardson / Photobus

Cap badge.
Viv Corbin collection

Preface

The mid-red buses used to sweep by with something approaching haughtiness. Picking-up restrictions meant they were not available to me; mundane trips to school and the shops had to be by Cardiff Corporation bus. Even the bus stops had an air of superiority about them. We had one nearby: they were big, framed, double-crown timetable posters. But Western Welsh buses were for more exotic trips to Barry or Penarth (although the latter could be a Corporation bus, albeit a rare single-decker). And they were everywhere. On our two-week family holiday to West Wales, there they were — same types, just different fleet numbers. I had my first full-time job with the company; it gave me a grounding in the bus industry that stood me in good stead throughout my career. In the early 'Seventies it all began to go very wrong, and the name change to the vague and inappropriate National Welsh in 1978 finished it once and for all. Very little remains: the huge Head Office site has disappeared under houses and a supermarket, while the routes are covered by an array of new companies. It is as if Western Welsh never existed. Calling on the enormous wealth of knowledge held by Chris Taylor and Viv Corbin, I hope this book will go some way towards redressing the balance.

Roger Davies
Leeds
July 2007

1. A Bit of Geography

From Hereford in the shire of the same name to Whitesands Bay near St David's in Pembrokeshire is a distance of some 110 miles, and from Aberystwyth in Cardiganshire to Barry Island in the far south of Glamorganshire is 80 miles. This large area of the United Kingdom was the operating territory of the British Electric Traction's Western Welsh Omnibus Company Limited. Few other bus companies in the UK can match that. And those that come near generally can have a claim to a substantial piece of the patch to themselves. Not so Western Welsh. Huge chunks of the area were denied it; for example, the big South Wales Transport Co, aided by United Welsh Services, saw to Swansea, whilst the major urban areas of Cardiff and Newport had their own Corporation fleets, and even in the centre of the Valleys, Pontypridd had its own fleet and was also served by yet another BET fleet, the Rhondda Transport Co. On top of that, no fewer than seven other Urban District Councils ran their own buses, additional BET companies looked after Port Talbot (Thomas Bros) and the key inter-urban Cardiff–Swansea route (Neath & Cardiff Luxury Coaches), and the big Red & White company was heavily involved in the eastern part of the area. If that were not enough, the patch enjoyed a high level of bus service provided by innumerable independents. To find towns that really belonged to Western Welsh you were looking at Bridgend and Barry, which, with all due respect, isn't a lot. And, although there were some joint services, Western Welsh tended to keep itself to itself: there were, until late on, no great, complex pooling arrangements over routes. Yet somehow a vast fleet of, at its peak, more than 700 buses, presented in a manner that put many others to shame and controlled from an imposing Head Office and works in suburban Cardiff, served this astonishing area. The more you think about it the more unusual it is. So how did it come about?

Did they all really get on board? Typical of the type of vehicle in the early days of what was to become Western Welsh was this Vulcan charabanc of June 1921, operated by T. Beavis of Risca. This was one of the predecessors of Danygraig Motor Services, taken over by WW in 1935. *Chris Taylor collection*

Lewis & James (Western Valleys) used the 'Blue Fleet Omnibus Services' name for a short time. Outside Risca Police Station in 1923, this ex-RAF Leyland has been fitted with the 'miracle' of wireless by Lush & Herrera of Crosskeys, hence the mighty structure on the roof. For the entertainment of passengers earphones were fitted to every seat, and it picked up the Cardiff station of the BBC, reception being reported as excellent. W. T. James recalled: "A full bus could be guaranteed during the time that the racing results were broadcast, passengers hopping off the bus at the next stop directly the bulletin was over." *Chris Taylor collection*

T. White & Co was an AEC agent for about four years before losing out to Romilly of Cardiff. It still bought many AECs; this vehicle, in grey coach livery, was one of its 'Y'-type charabancs of 1922. *Chris Taylor collection*

In absolutely superb condition is the former WW 631, a Brush-bodied AEC Regent II working for Yeoman's of Hereford and seen in that city's bus station. This is appropriate, as Hereford was as far east as Western Welsh got, albeit not for long, on a rail-replacement service from Brecon. *John Wiltshire*

A general view of Bridgend bus station and the largest depot in the summer of 1962, featuring Atlanteans of all three batches delivered thus far, there being detail differences. You can also see the distinctive twin lower-deck rear windows. There's also a Bridgemaster, a Regent V, a selection of saloons and a typical crew. Just visible behind 333 is the distinctive rear end of a Weymann bus body, with three windows (on account of the emergency door). Western Welsh had hordes of these, and for many motorists this was the typical image of the company! *Tony Warrener*

2. Mine's a Pint

Albert Gray.
Christine Davies collection

Let's start in Wiveliscombe, in Somerset. The Hancock family came from there, and in 1805 William of that ilk started to brew beer on his own account. His son, also William, expanded the business, and by 1871 brothers Joseph and William Gaskell had joined in and were acting as agents in the rapidly expanding South Wales market based in Bute West Dock, Cardiff. In 1883 the Hancocks decided to brew in Cardiff, buying up the Bute Dock Brewery, and in 1894 expanded by purchasing the County Brewery in Penarth Road and Crawshay Street. During all these years the Gaskell family were not only deeply involved in the business but also had a close association with the military, particularly the Territorial Army. By 1905, to distribute their wares they had put on the road a Dennis lorry, followed by Milnes-Daimlers. Thus in the early part of the 20th century, like many in this industry, they had accumulated experience in motorised transport and were making decent profits.

Following World War 1 the brewery decided to build on this base and to assist with the employment of trained drivers no longer required by the Armed Forces. Having no work for them, it established a subsidiary — South Wales Commercial Motors — in May 1919. Albert Gray was appointed General Manager, initiating something of a dynasty. Born in 1879, he had joined Hancocks as Transport Manager in 1906, having started his career in Birmingham and served his apprenticeship with a steam engine company before moving to Wolverhampton to join the Star Cycle Company (which back in 1897 had built its first petrol-driven car) and then back to Birmingham with the Ariel Motor Company. With this background Albert was just the right man for the job: being passionately interested in things mechanical, he already had several engineering patents to his name and envisaged a great future for buses. His grand-daughter, Christine Davies, recalls that beside his chair at home he had a large metal box in which he kept drawings and plans of all his ideas.

A group of SCWM staff gathered around an early Commer.
Christine Davies collection

On 1 July 1919 Ernest S. Mountain joined as Works Manager, and tenancy was taken of 8/8A Penarth Road, which brought with it a large recreational hall, and other buildings in Crawshay Street. Early in 1920 SWCM took on a sales and service agreement for Commer, by now Hancocks' preferred make of vehicle; this was achieved by purchasing shares in a company called Commercial Cars Ltd. Then, on 1 April, at 10am, the company started its first bus service, between Cardiff and

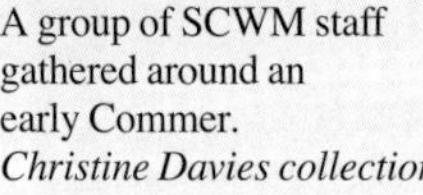

the nearby, rather smart coastal town of Penarth. There was an historical link too, one of the Hancock family having been a director of the Penarth Promenade & Landing Pier Co in 1888. Understandably, Commer buses were chosen, early examples being chain-driven. These pioneering buses were pretty basic, and spares always carried included a length of string, a roll of wire and a can of water. Sometimes conductors had to lie along the mudguard to flood the carburettor to get the bus back, and it was unusual for a whole day to pass without some trouble. Nevertheless, those early drivers took great pride in their 'horses',

◄ The start of it all in 1920: SWCM No 1, a chain-driven Commer RC, probably ex War Department. It has what looks like a brewer's-dray cab and what Albert Gray described as a 'horse-tram body', although what horse trams were around then is a good question. A picture of this vehicle, rebodied as a charabanc, on the Newport–Chepstow route graced the wall of Cowbridge Road office, and a fine model of it, along with a Lion and a Tiger Cub, adorned the foyer. Like so much of the company it probably ended up in a skip. The bus later passed to Eastern Valleys. *Chris Taylor collection*

◄ No 2 was another Commer RC. Livery was red, with white above the windows, and the fleetname was believed to be the largest in the country! Cardiff Corporation's Watch Committee issued numbers to the vehicles of all licensed operators, and this had to be carried prominently, as did fleet numbers. No 2 was No 35. Everyone got very confused. *Chris Taylor collection*

What appears to be a Corpus Christi procession winds its way down Penarth Road towards Cardiff General station in the early 1920s. Leading is a well-loaded BO 4131, an SWCM Commer charabanc. This vehicle was sold in 1921 but, due to a default in payments, repurchased in 1922. *Viv Corbin collection*

as they were known, and could often be found in their leisure time polishing them. Or should that be grooming?

On 23 November 1920 the company was formally registered as South Wales Commercial Motors Ltd, with a capital of £20,000 in £1 shares and four directors — Colonel J. Gaskell as Chairman, Major J. G. Gaskell and A. Gray as joint Managing Directors and W. T. Wilkes as Company Secretary. Each was allocated 5,000 shares and received a salary of £250 per annum.

The early 1920s was a time of tremendous growth in bus services. In December 1920 SWCM started a service westwards from Cardiff to Cowbridge, and in the same month Barry Urban District Council granted a licence to run to that town. In February 1921 a two-hourly service started to Dinas Powys, soon being extended through to Barry. In March the Cowbridge service was extended further west, to Bridgend, where an office was rented for five years at 1 Market Street, and a garage opened for seven buses at Free School Lane. The latter was soon outgrown, and a larger garage, for 12 buses, in Brackla Road was rented for five years at £130 per annum. Things were moving apace in other parts too: by 12 April an hourly service was running to Barry, and 13 days later a route began linking Newport with Chepstow, running from a rented garage in Charlotte Street, Newport. However, things were not easy, and, in order to protect its own local tram services, Newport Corporation denied SWCM the right to run from the town centre, the company's buses having to start from the trams' outer termini. The company appealed to the Ministry of Transport, and the Corporation reluctantly agreed, with conditions, to allow buses to start from Alfred Street/Church Street from 22 April 1922, only to withdraw the licence eight months later. Following public meetings the Corporation finally agreed to a terminus at Skinner Street in April 1923, moving it to Rodney Street from 14 May. That month, in Maesteg, north of Bridgend, SWCM sought to avoid confrontation by offering to pay the local council one penny per road mile operated through its area. Under the Roads Act 1920 the company was not obliged to do so, and it was shortly revealed that the council should not have accepted the payment. Such were the perils of early bus operation!

Back in 1921 there was a significant development that was to be an aspect of the company for many years. This was a parcel

This photograph was taken from the first floor of the SWCM offices at 8A Crawshay Street, Cardiff. Perhaps the smartly uniformed drivers are changing over on one of the company's Commer charabancs.
Viv Corbin collection

Col. J. GASKELL — Mr. A. GRAY
Major J. G. GASKELL — Mr. W. T. WILKES
Wish each Member of the South Wales Commercial Motors Ltd.
A very Happy Xmas and a Prosperous New Year.

Mr. A. David — Xmas 1920.

This Christmas card was presented to employees and customers of the newly formed SCWM. At the end of 1920 there were about 45 employees and the weekly wage bill was around £200. The Commer saloon, L 6471, was used on the Cardiff–Cowbridge service, which was extended to Bridgend in 1921. Van No 2 was sold to Mr W. Evans in July 1921 for £1,000. *Viv Corbin collection*

▲ The fleet in Bridgend in the early 1920s — a mix of Commer RC saloons and 3P charabancs. Drivers' motorcycles are in evidence, as is a Newport-registered 'Cyclecar' — a type that had a great following around this time. *Chris Taylor collection*

service that commenced in August. In command was Inspector Albert E. Smith, who had started his career preparing and publishing the company's timetables. 'Advertisements were canvassed … I went around personally and convinced businessmen that the timetable would be an excellent medium, and when these were obtained I collated them with the timetable information, made them into a booklet, took them to a printer and arranged for their distribution. The booklet was modestly priced at one penny, and it sold very well,' he recalled in later years. Those involved in publicising buses today could learn much from Inspector Smith!

The same year saw services starting from Bridgend to Porthcawl on the coast and up into the Rhondda to reach Pontypridd. The establishment of Bridgend as a firm base continued apace following the appointment from 21 November of Captain G. T. Willcox as Manager, at £350 per annum. In 1922 land was leased for a bus station, and routes were initiated to Caerau, Blaengarw and

◄ All ready for the Newport–Chepstow route, a Commer bodied by SWCM is checked over by the Police outside Penarth Police Station before entering service in June 1920. This bus would be sold in March 1925 to become a lorry. *Chris Taylor collection*

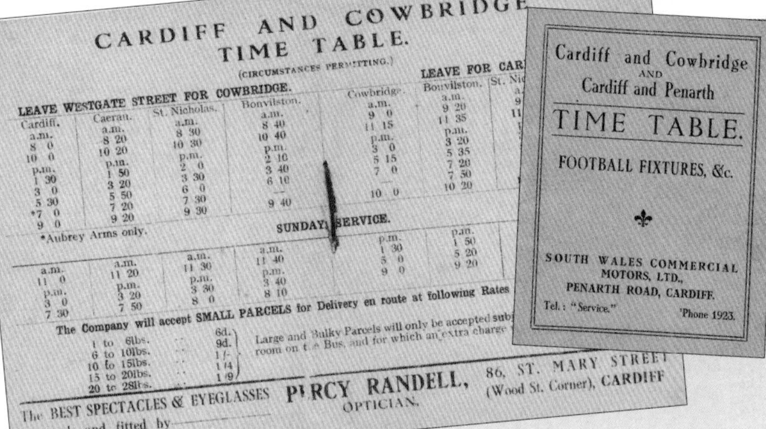

CARDIFF AND COWBRIDGE
TIME TABLE.
(CIRCUMSTANCES PERMITTING.)

LEAVE WESTGATE STREET FOR COWBRIDGE. / LEAVE FOR CAR[DIFF]

Cardiff.	Caerau.	St. Nicholas.	Bonvilston.	Cowbridge.	Bonvilston.
a.m.	a.m.	a.m.	a.m.	a.m.	a.m.
8 0	8 20	8 30	8 40	9 0	9 20
10 0	10 20	10 30	10 40	11 15	11 35
p.m.	p.m.	p.m.	p.m.	p.m.	p.m.
1 30	1 50	2 0	2 10	3 0	3 20
3 0	3 20	3 30	3 40	5 15	5 35
5 30	5 50	6 0	6 10	7 0	7 20
*7 0	7 20	7 30	—	—	7 50
9 0	9 20	9 30	9 40	10 0	10 20

*Aubrey Arms only.

SUNDAY SERVICE.

Cardiff.	Caerau.	St. Nicholas.	Bonvilston.	Cowbridge.	Bonvilston.
a.m.	a.m.	a.m.	a.m.	p.m.	p.m.
11 0	11 20	11 30	11 40	1 30	1 50
p.m.	p.m.	p.m.	p.m.		
3 0	3 20	3 30	3 40	5 0	5 20
7 30	7 50	8 0	8 10	9 0	9 20

The Company will accept SMALL PARCELS for Delivery en route at following Rates

1 to 6lbs.	6d.
6 to 10lbs.	9d.
10 to 15lbs.	1/-
15 to 20lbs.	1/4
20 to 28lbs.	1/9

Large and Bulky Parcels will only be accepted sub[ject to] room on the Bus, and for which an extra charge [...]

The BEST SPECTACLES & EYEGLASSES are made and fitted by PERCY RANDELL, OPTICIAN. 86, ST. MARY STREET (Wood St. Corner), CARDIFF

Cardiff and Cowbridge
AND
Cardiff and Penarth
TIME TABLE.
FOOTBALL FIXTURES, &c.
SOUTH WALES COMMERCIAL MOTORS, LTD.,
PENARTH ROAD, CARDIFF.
Tel.: "Service." 'Phone 1923.

CARDIFF, COWBRIDGE, AND BRIDGEND, connecting with PORTHCAWL, MAESTEG, AND OGMORE VALE.

WEEK-DAYS.

		am	am	am	pm	pm	pm	pm	pm	pm
Cardiff (Westgate Street).	dep.	..	8. 0	10. 0	..	1.30	3. 0	5.30	7. 0	9. 0
Caerau	,,	..	8.20	10.20	..	1.50	3.20	5.50	7.20	9.20
St. Nicholas	,,	..	8.30	10.30	..	2. 0	3.30	6. 0	7.30	9.30
Bonvilston	,,	..	8.40	10.40	..	2.10	3.40	6.10	7.40	9.40
Cowbridge	,,	..	9. 0	11. 0	..	2.30	4. 0	6.30	8. 0	10. 0
Penllyn Crossing	,,	..	9. 8	11. 8	..	2.38	4. 8	6.38	8. 8	10. 8
Colwinstone	,,	..	9.10	11.10	..	2.40	4.10	6.40	8.10	10.10
Brocastle	,,	..	9.15	11.15	..	2.45	4.15	6.45	8.15	10.15
Bridgend	arr.	..	9.30	11.30	..	3. 0	4.30	7. 0	8.30	10.30
Bridgend	dep.	..	9.30	11.30	..	3.30	4.30	7.30	8.30	..
Porthcawl	arr.	..	10. 0	12. 0	..	4. 0	5. 0	8. 0	9. 0	..
Porthcawl	dep.	..	10.15	12.15	2.15	4.15	6.15	8. 0	9.15	..
Bridgend	arr.	..	10.45	12.45	2.45	4.45	6.45	8.30	9.45	..
Bridgend	dep.	..	9.30	12. 0	..	3. 0	4.30	7. 0	9. 0	..
Maesteg	arr.	..	10.25	12.55	..	3.55	5.25	7.55	9.55	..
Maesteg	dep.	..	9.30	12. 0	2. 0	4. 0	5.30	7.30	10. 0	..
Bridgend	arr.	..	10.25	12.55	2.55	4.55	6.25	8.25	10.55	..
Bridgend	dep.	..	10.30	1. 0	..	3.30	6.30	..	8.30	..
Ogmore Vale	arr.	..	11.15	1.45	..	4.15	7.15	..	9.15	..
Ogmore Vale	dep.	..	9.40	11.55	2.10	..	5.10	7.40	9.40	..
Bridgend	arr.	..	10.25	12.45	2.55	..	5.55	8.25	10.25	..
Bridgend	dep.	8.30	10.45	1. 0	3. 0	5. 0	7. 0	8.30	..	..
Brocastle Cros'g	,,	8.40	10.55	1.10	3.10	5.10	7.10	8.40	..	..
Colwinstone	,,	8.45	11. 0	1.15	3.15	5.15	7.15	8.45	..	..
Penllyn	,,	8.50	11. 5	1.20	3.20	5.20	7.20	8.50	..	..
Cowbridge	,,	9. 0	11.15	1.30	3.30	5.30	7.30	9.0	..	..
Bonvilston	,,	9.20	11.35	1.50	3.50	5.50	7.50	9.[illegible]	..	..
St. Nicholas	,,	9.30	11.45	2. 0	4.0	6. 0	8. 0	9.[illegible]	..	..
Caerau	,,	9.40	11.55	2.10	4.10	6.10	8.10	9.[illegible]	..	..
Cardiff	arr.	10. 0	12.15	2.30	4.30	6.30	8.30	10[illegible]	..	..

SUNDAYS.

		am	am	pm
Cardiff (Westgate Street).	dep.	..	10.30	..
Caerau	,,	..	10.50	..
St. Nicholas	,,	..	11. 0	..
Bonvilston	,,	..	11.10	..
Cowbridge	,,	..	11.30	..
Penllyn Crossing	,,	..	11.38	..
Colwinstone	,,	..	11.40	..
Brocastle	,,	..	11.45	..
Bridgend	arr.	..	12. 0	..
Bridgend	dep.	..	12. 0	..
Porthcawl	arr.	..	12.30	..
Porthcawl	dep.	10.30	12.45	2. 0
Bridgend	arr.	11. 0	1.15	2.30
Bridgend	dep.	..	12. 0	..
Maesteg	arr.	..	12.55	..
Maesteg	dep.	10. 0	12.30	1.3[illegible]
Bridgend	arr.	10.55	1.25	2.2[illegible]
Bridgend	dep.	..	..	..
Ogmore Vale	arr.	..	..	..
Ogmore Vale	dep.	10.10	12.40	[illegible]
Bridgend	arr.	10.55	1.25	[illegible]
Bridgend	dep.	11. 0	1.30	2.[illegible]
Brocastle Cros'g	,,	11.10	1.40	2.[illegible]
Colwinstone	,,	11.15	1.45	2[illegible]
Penllyn	,,	11.20	1.50	2[illegible]
Cowbridge	,,	11.30	2. 0	3[illegible]
Bonvilston	,,	11.50	2.20	3[illegible]
St. Nicholas	,,	12. 0	2.30	3.30
Caerau	,,	12.10	2.40	3.40
Cardiff	arr.	12.30	3. 0	4. 0

TIME TABLE
Motor Bus Services
CARDIFF
TO
Cowbridge, Maesteg, Bridgend, Ogmore Vale, Porthcawl, Penarth, and Barry Island.
SOUTH WALES COMMERCIAL MOTORS, LD.
Tel.: "Service." 'Phone 1923.
The Educational Publishing Co., Ltd., Cardiff

First timetables — the handiwork of Inspector Albert E. Smith. *Christine Davies collection*

▼ The bus station in Bridgend that opened in 1922, likely making it the first in Wales and one of the first three in the UK. On the left is a charabanc heading for Southerndown. These were a nightmare for conductors. Fares had to be collected from the running-board as the bus was in motion, albeit at only 12mph, at least officially! With tickets in one hand and money in the other, hanging on by elbow alone, the conductor had to hope the door was locked (which it often wasn't). The wheel arch presented the greatest difficulty: there was no foothold, and the span was too great for the short-legged! These were high-frame vehicles, and a short ladder had to be provided for passengers to board and alight. On top of all this was what was laughably described as a 'one-man hood', supported by bamboo struts that fitted into slots in the top of the bodywork; it was not uncommon to see driver, conductor and several passengers struggling with this in a rainstorm! The other bus displays Albert Gray's patented sliding roof, a great improvement. *Christine Davies colelction*

3

PARCEL DELIVERY SERVICE.

The Company give notice that they have established a Parcel Office in almost every town or village covered by the Motor Bus Service, where parcels can now be accepted for delivery by Motor Bus or handed to Conductors on Buses at the following rates, at owner's risk:—

Weight not exceeding		Weight not exceeding	
6 lbs. ..	4d.	56 lbs. ..	1/4
10 lbs. ..	6d.	75 lbs. ..	1/6
16 lbs. ..	9d.	112 lbs. ..	1/9
28 lbs. ..	1/–		

All Parcels to be prepaid.

All parcels for Penarth can be handed to Conductors on Buses at Terminus, St. Mary Street, Cardiff, or Company's Office, Penarth Road.

Parcels for Cowbridge, Bridgend and all places beyond can be left at Mr. I. C. GRIFFITHS, 13, Quay Street, or Company's Office, Penarth Road.

Buses leave Westgate Street every hour from 8 a.m. until 10 p.m.

The Company also give notice that they are not common carriers, and will under no circumstances be held responsible for breakages, loss, or theft of parcels whilst in their care, accompanied or unaccompanied by the owner, and parcels are only accepted for transit on the Company's Omnibuses on these conditions.

All parcels will receive our prompt attention, and quick despatch is assured.

Parcel-delivery details.
Viv Corbin collection

The Commer 3P was a fairly old design with a straight chassis frame. SWCM designed a body to give the impression of a lower vehicle. Note the low window line and camel roof; also that the mudguards are brought down low and joined up. The rear entrance, Scottish-style, had a lowered extension. These bodies were built by SWCM and by the Cardiff-registered firm of Northern Counties Motor & Engineering (NCME); this is one of the latter's products on a Daimler chassis, exhibited at the 1925 Commercial Motor Show.
Chris Taylor collection

The attraction! Barry Island in the early 1920s, with one of several Vulcan 'Blackpools' with a local operator. From the 1960s a Butlin's holiday camp would dominate the headland for more than 30 years but has since been demolished.
Chris Taylor collection

Ogmore Vale. The bus station opened later that year, and from November a certain Mrs Hinton, who was to stay for many years, opened up a refreshment room. These were very competitive times, and Mr Willcox, Mr E. Rees (who succeeded him in 1923) and their loyal team fought hard to keep the gains they made and build the foundation of what was to become the company's largest depot. However, the company was not so astute over the other place that was ultimately to figure considerably, for in August 1922 it informed Barry UDC that its licences in the town were no longer required. Barry grew into a major and popular seaside resort, at one stage in 1924 supporting (amongst other things) no fewer than 45 bus companies, so it was a decision regretted for many years as the company tried desperately to regain these routes.

Despite all this activity, Mr Gray found time to patent a sliding roof design for single-deck buses. This was taken up in April 1924 by bodybuilder Northern Counties Motor & Engineering, which, although based in Wigan, was always registered in Cardiff. In the meantime Inspector Smith had not been idle, the parcels service reporting a profit of £253 in its first year.

In March 1923 the company became an agent for Lancia, but a month later Commercial Cars Ltd, the Commer dealership, was put into

This was where you caught the Penarth bus in Cardiff until the opening of the bus station in 1954. The Commer has a hinged opening entrance door, and tram poles are still in place along the centre of St Mary Street.
Chris Taylor collection

PRICE ONE PENNY.

TRAVEL BY ROAD

South Wales Commercial Motors, Ld.

MOTOR BUS SERVICES TIME TABLE

From OCTOBER, 1923, and until further notice

Head Office: PENARTH ROAD, CARDIFF.
Telegrams, "Service," Cardiff. Telephone, 1923.

Branch Office: MARKET ST., BRIDGEND.
Telephone, 189 Bridgend.

The Educational Publishing Co., Ltd., Cardiff.

SWCM timetable, 1923, with the patented roof again.
Viv Corbin collection

receivership. Despite this it entered into an agency agreement with Leyland in 1925 and continued to trade until 1926, when it was bought by Humber, and went on to become part of the Rootes Group. Meanwhile, in April 1923, SWCM introduced a seasonal service from Bridgend around the dramatic coastline to Southerndown, and private hires, using charabancs, were advertised. These latter did not prove as successful as hoped, and the vehicles often appeared on local bus services.

Certainly things didn't all go SWCM's way. An application for a licence from Bridgend to Kenfig Hill via the ridge, 450ft above sea level, that is Cefn Cribbwr, and well populated into the bargain, was refused, as the Cridlands company already served it. Undeterred, SWCM started a service via Aberkenfig — which still brought it into competition with Cridlands — in April 1924. In the same month a 21-year lease was signed for the Armoury Garage, Cowbridge, and in October a new depot was completed in Talbot Green (then known as Green Talbot), for £309. Having by now realised the error of its ways, the company requested new licences from Barry UDC. They were refused.

January 1925 proved eventful following the extension of the Cardiff–Penarth service to the town boundary at Lower Penarth. Within days White's Motor Co of Barry started to compete over the new section of route and from 13 April over the entire route, running as a Barry–Wenvoe–Cardiff–Penarth–Barry circular. From the following month the route saw yet more competition in the form of Cardiff Corporation, with which SWCM had entered into a joint timetable agreement — though not with White's! Nevertheless the route remained the company's most profitable, followed by that to Bridgend and routes thence to Pontypridd and Maesteg.

By the end of the year the fleet stood at around 35 buses, garaged in Bridgend, Cardiff, Caerwent, Cowbridge, Llanharan, Newport, Pontycymmer, Porthcawl and Talbot Green.

In May 1926 the Cardiff–Bridgend route was strengthened when competitor A. Maddox of Cowbridge, with two buses, was bought out, for £1,400. He also owned a fish-and-chip shop in the town! A garage in Kenfig Hill was bought for £240, showing commitment to this area, and further expansion took place on the Bridgend site.

The General Strike saw the company's buses running on local services in Cardiff. On one occasion a member of staff was told off for chalking the destination 'Whitchurch' on a new Commer! Postage stamps were collected in lieu of fares, and buses and crews returned to Bridgend overnight.

As the year drew to a close SWCM once again reached Barry, this time from Bridgend via Bonvilston. Over this period the vehicle-purchasing policy had been mainly Commer and Lancia, but many vehicles, notably Leylands, had joined the fleet through acquisitions.

At the end of 1926 the company reported total profits of £16,583 over the previous six years but that recent profit levels had been hit by customers' failing to meet their hire-purchase payments on vehicles. The bank overdraft stood at £4,000, and Hancocks was looking for cash to purchase a brewery. This state of affairs no doubt influenced the April 1927 sale of the company to The National Electric Construction Co (which also owned, amongst others, Rhondda, Devon General and City of Oxford), for five shillings a share. The Press, as ever wide of the mark, thought that SWCM was being taken over by Rhondda, although the Manager of that company, Mr T. G. Richardson, did become a SWCM director.

It was last orders for Hancocks.

▲ The bus that made all previous vehicles obsolete was the Leyland Lion PLSC1. No 5 is here posed on the climb up from Penarth promenade, presumably on a trail run. Note the pier in the background. New in February 1926, this was the first Lion in South Wales. *Chris Taylor collection*

South Wales Commercial Motors, Ld.

Up-to-date First-class Charabanc and Saloon Cars for Hire.

Comfortable and Easy Riding.

Private Parties, Outings, Club Meetings, Picnic Parties, Dances, etc.

Any Number Catered for.

Write or Telephone for Particulars.

Head Office: PENARTH ROAD, CARDIFF.

Branch Office: 1, MARKET STREET, BRIDGEND.

Telephones: 1923 Cardiff, and 169 Bridgend.

◂◂ Charabanc hire leaflet 1922; not very successful! *Viv Corbin collection*

BRIDGEND AND SOUTHERNDOWN. TABLE OF FARES.

From / To	Bridgend	White Rock.	Ewenny.	Pelican Inn.	Portabelo	Sutton	Ogmore Cafe.	South'n-down
Bridgend ..	—	2d.	3d.	5d.	6d.	8d.	9d.	11d.
White Rock ..	2d.	—	2d.	4d.	5d.	7d.	8d.	10d.
Ewenny ..	3d.	2d.	—	2d.	3d.	5d.	6d.	8d.
Pelican Inn	5d.	4d.	2d.	—	2d.	3d.	4d.	6d.
Portabelo ..	6d.	5d.	3d.	2d.	—	2d.	3d.	5d.
Sutton ..	8d.	7d.	5d.	3d.	2d.	—	2d.	3d.
Ogmore Cafe	9d.	8d.	6d.	4d.	3d.	2d.	—	2d.
Southerndown	11d.	10d.	8d.	6d.	5d.	3d.	2d.	—

Children over 4 and under 14, Half-fares.
All Parcels for Southerndown will be left at Verity's Cafe until called for.
For Cheap Return Fares, see Pages 28 and 29.

THE NEST
OGMORE-BY-SEA

A HOME FROM HOME for first-class Teas, Refreshments, Hot or Cold Lunches, etc. Home-made Cakes and Pastries supplied. Large or Small Touring Parties, School Outings, etc., catered for. Moderate Terms. Every comfort for Board-Residents. Facing Sea.

Telephone: Southerndown 29.

L. C. BAMON, Proprietress.

◂ Fares to Southerndown, 1929. *Viv Corbin collection*

3. A Brief Interlude

One of the original Lewis & James buses that started the Western Valleys services was No 4, an ex-RAF Leyland fitted with a new 32-seat body. This mighty beast was the start of a fleet that grew rapidly and was mostly of Leyland manufacture. *Chris Taylor collection*

The Board resigned, and a new Board, headed by Chairman and Managing Director W. B. Cownie, already Managing Director of Rhondda Tramways in Porth, took over. His first action was to tell staff that they would get three weeks' extra money if a profit were made in 1927! Mr A. Gray happily survived the changes to become General Manager on £750 per annum, but Ernest Mountain, the Works Manager, resigned. The registered office became 62/63 Queen Street in London.

No doubt in the light of SWCM's recent experiences, the new Board's policy was to scale down the motor and sales side whilst expanding the successful bus business. It wasted no time, and the significant Lewis & James business of Newbridge, which traded as Western Valleys, was bought almost straightaway, for £25,250, although the agreement was not finalised until 10 November. L&J had been in negotiation with Newport Corporation, but this was broken off. The deal brought about 25 buses of ADC, AEC, Albion and Leyland manufacture and routes in the Western Valleys of Monmouthshire and linking into Newport, which would soon be expanded to serve Cardiff and Ebbw Vale. Indeed, under NECC patronage the company grew, even running a service to Aberystwyth via Brecon, the licence for which was held by the Great Western Railway. There was even a suggestion of closer links with Rhondda Transport, which put 'Newport' on its blinds but never got there! Western Valleys had been weakened by the establishment by the Bedwellty and Mynyddislwyn councils of their own bus operation, the West Monmouthshire Omnibus Board, and almost had the same thing happen in Risca and Abercarn, but the proposal was defeated at a plebiscite. The two partners stayed on, W. T. James rising through the BET ranks, and J. H. Lewis becoming Chief Engineer of Western Welsh upon its formation but leaving later after an argument; he became a haulier and dealer in Foden trucks. In November Mr Cownie resigned, being replaced by one Harley C. Drayton. In December Barry Council again refused SWCM licences from Cardiff, so the company took to transferring passengers from the

In 1925 Western Valleys took over the Sirhowy Valleys fleet. The company was renamed for a while as shown, but in October 1926 the Sirhowy fleet was purchased by the West Mon Omnibus Board. This vehicle, AX 9616, was a Saurer with Dodson 30-seat bodywork that was bought for a proposed route up and down Aberbargoed Hill, which involved steep gradients and sharp bends. It passed to West Mon, which is more readily associated with this route. *Chris Taylor collection*

SCWM letterhead of 1927, showing a map and the dealerships. *Viv Corbin collection*

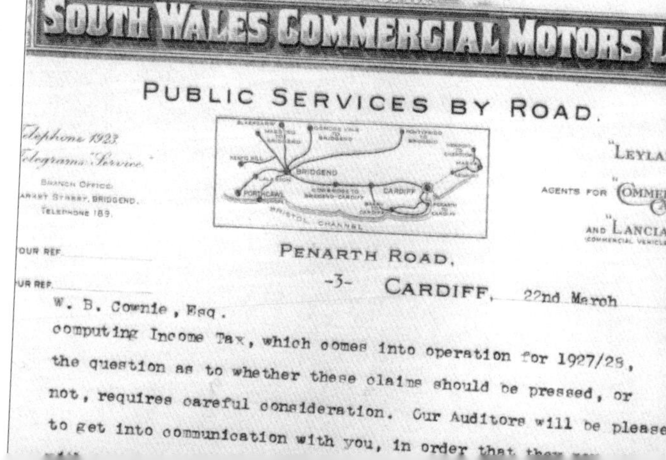

SOUTH WALES COMMERCIAL MOTORS L

PUBLIC SERVICES BY ROAD.

Telephone 1923
Telegrams "Service."
Branch Office:
...arket Street, Bridgend.
Telephone 189.

"LEYLA...
AGENTS FOR "COMME...
AND "LANCIA"
COMMERCIAL VEHICLE...

...OUR REF.
...UR REF.

PENARTH ROAD,
-3- CARDIFF, 22nd March

W. B. Cownie, Esq.

computing Income Tax, which comes into operation for 1927/28, the question as to whether these claims should be pressed, or not, requires careful consideration. Our Auditors will be please... to get into communication with you, in order that they ...

Pictured at Sycamore Cross, not far from St Nicholas and where connections were made to Barry, is No 39 (BT 8432), an all-Leyland SG11 new in May 1925. It was purchased from Leah & Beulah and fitted with pneumatic tyres, allowing an increase in licensed speed from 12 to 20mph. The height of this straightforward chassis made it obsolete very quickly. *Chris Taylor collection*

Cardiff–Bridgend route onto the Bridgend–Barry service where they met at Sycamore Cross. This was not popular in the corridors of power in Barry! In July 1927 the Newport–Chepstow service was sold to a private individual, ultimately passing to Red & White. A loss of £5,046 for the year 1926/7 suggests action had been taken just in time.

In February 1928 share issue was raised to £150,000. In that month also another significant purchase was made, for £41,000, namely Barrett Bros (trading as Eastern Valleys) of Pontnewydd, a significant SWCM customer for chassis. This brought around 27 buses of Commer, ADC, AEC and Leyland manufacture and routes in the Blaenavon, Pontypool and Newport areas. Both this and Western Valleys were kept separate from SWCM, although there was a lot of inter-linking, and the running receipts were reported in June 1928 as 10.10 pence per mile for SWCM, 11.81 for Western Valleys and 9.19 for Eastern. In August £4,500 was paid for the five buses of Lancia, Leyland and Thornycroft manufacture that made up the business of J. Jones & Co of Pontycymmer, trading as Garw Transport, with routes in the Bridgend area and to Blaengarw. In the same month SWCM's Head Office, along with all others in the NECC group, moved to Salisbury Square House in London. All this seemed to work, a profit for the year of £3,102 being recorded for the group's 119 buses.

Western Valleys moved on to ADCs, and its last batch were 416/2 models with Northern Counties bodywork featuring Scottish-style entrances. New in May 1928, they became Western Welsh 213-9. *Chris Taylor collection*

Eastern Valleys No 42 was a Dennis Lancet with a Weymann body, one of four new in 1932. It became Western Welsh 355, not needing much livery change, as the two were similar. It would be sold quite early, in March 1940. *Chris Taylor collection*

4. It's the Railways, Stupid !

Early WW timetable.
Viv Corbin collection

Typical of the small buses used by the GWR, this was one of 40 similar Thornycroft A1s with 19-seat bodies built by the same firm and delivered in 1925. It featured the reliable 22.4hp FB4 side-valve engine which made the A1 a popular choice with many South Wales operators. Numbered 919 by the GWR, it became Western Welsh 424 in October 1933 and was used at Pontypool before withdrawal in 1935.
Kenneth Evans collection

Over the years the GWR had been introducing feeder bus services to its rail services. In South and West Wales and in Monmouthshire it had built up an extensive network using more than 90 buses, mainly of Guy and Maudslay manufacture but including some Thornycrofts and a few odds and ends. Such was the spread that routes were grouped into areas — Aberdare (eight routes), Brecon (eight), Abergavenny (eight), Neath (12) and West Wales (15) — and stretched from Hay-on-Wye in the east to Cardigan and St David's in the west. Whilst four predated the war, the earliest (linking New Quay with Llandysul) having started on 1 May 1907, most had grown up in the late 1920s. Nine had been taken over from other operators, and seven were jointly operated. On 27 March 1929 agreement was reached with SWCM with its 60 buses for the GWR to take a 50% stake in a new company formed to merge the bus services of both. As a result, on 17 May, share issue was raised to £500,000, and a public company was set up on 3 June. After several titles, including 'Great Western Omnibus Company' and 'Great Gwalia Omnibus Company', had been rejected, the name 'Western Welsh' was selected. It's the railway 'Western', see, not geographical, although the GWR did provide westerly expansion. It was this move that formed the huge operating area, far in excess of what SWCM could reasonably have expected to achieve on its own and a feature that gave the company its unique character. It is also significant that the GWR, much the larger partner, did not take more of a commanding role in the new enterprise and that, had it not been for some reluctance on the part of SWCM, Aberystwyth would have come in too! The GWR regretted that, whilst holding a major share, it did not have much influence on the new company.

Early Trojan parcels van.
Viv Corbin collection

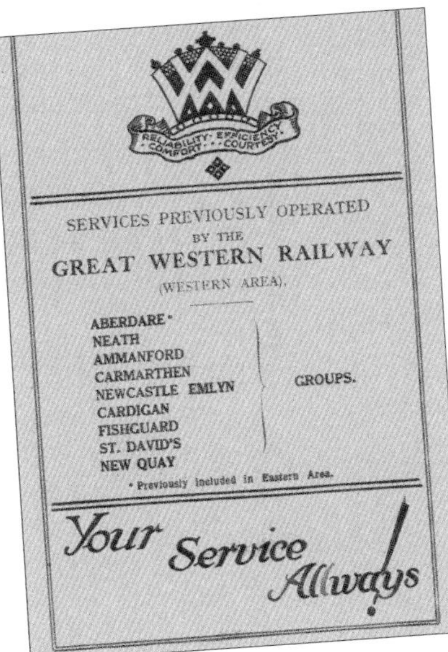
RELIABILITY · EFFICIENCY · COMFORT · COURTESY

SERVICES PREVIOUSLY OPERATED
BY THE
GREAT WESTERN RAILWAY
(WESTERN AREA).

ABERDARE*
NEATH
AMMANFORD
CARMARTHEN
NEWCASTLE EMLYN
CARDIGAN
FISHGUARD
ST. DAVID'S
NEW QUAY

GROUPS.

* Previously included in Eastern Area.

Your Service Always!

◂◂ WW timetable from 1929, showing ex-GWR services. *Viv Corbin collection*

◂ Cardiff Watch Committee No 47 was a Dennis 4-tonner with Dodson 52-seat body, new to Cridlands in 1924. It was used on the Cardiff–Pontypridd service but suffered so much from broken half-shafts that spares were carried on the bus! It became Western Welsh No 78 in November 1929, was converted to lorry No 1 in March 1934 and was sold for £2 10s 0d (£2.50) in August 1935. *Chris Taylor collection*

◂ Dating from 1927, WW 1278 was a Guy FBB with Vickers 32-seat rear-entrance bodywork that was typical of the GWR fleet. Cliff Wiltshire from Ely Head Office recalled that the engine fell out of one when in service — no wonder WW wasn't impressed! *Chris Taylor collection*

Amongst the new appointments we find the return of W. B. Cownie as Managing Director, while Albert Gray's abilities ensured that he continued as General Manager despite being up against GWR staff for his job. The new company was not slow to begin expansion by acquisition. Competitor H. J. Cridland was bought on 1 November for £33,000, bringing routes in Cardiff and Port Talbot and a fleet of 21 mainly Leyland and Daimler buses. On the same date the associated Tresillian Motors of Cardiff brought seven buses — a mixture of AEC, Daimler and Dennis vehicles — for £6,500. The takeover of former GWR garages — a gradual process that makes it difficult to be specific about what went on and when — continued, with only Glyncorrwg, Cardigan, Haverfordwest and Llandysul outstanding at the year end. However, Guy buses were not popular, and, despite the replacement of the originals with new Conquest models, few vehicles of this make survived beyond 1935. Ex-GWR buses generally retained their fleet numbers, and the system of classes — as with railway locomotives — would be maintained throughout the existence of Western Welsh.

The new team must have been pleased to report a profit of £6,466 over the year and early in 1930, for £2,300, purchased 8 acres of land on Cowbridge Road in Ely, Cardiff, on which to build a workshop and office complex. Owing to the way the company had grown, repair and overhaul of the fleet was carried out independently at several outlying depots. 'Such a condition of affairs was far from satisfactory, entailing a great deal of unnecessary work to obtain proper co-operation,' claimed J. H. Lewis. 'The establishment of a large and up-to-date central works where the whole fleet can be overhauled is obviously demanded.'

The 1930 Road Traffic Act sought to bring order to the bus industry, requiring operators to license services and fares with a new authority, the Traffic Commissioner, who would have powers to punish those who transgressed. Whilst viewing the new

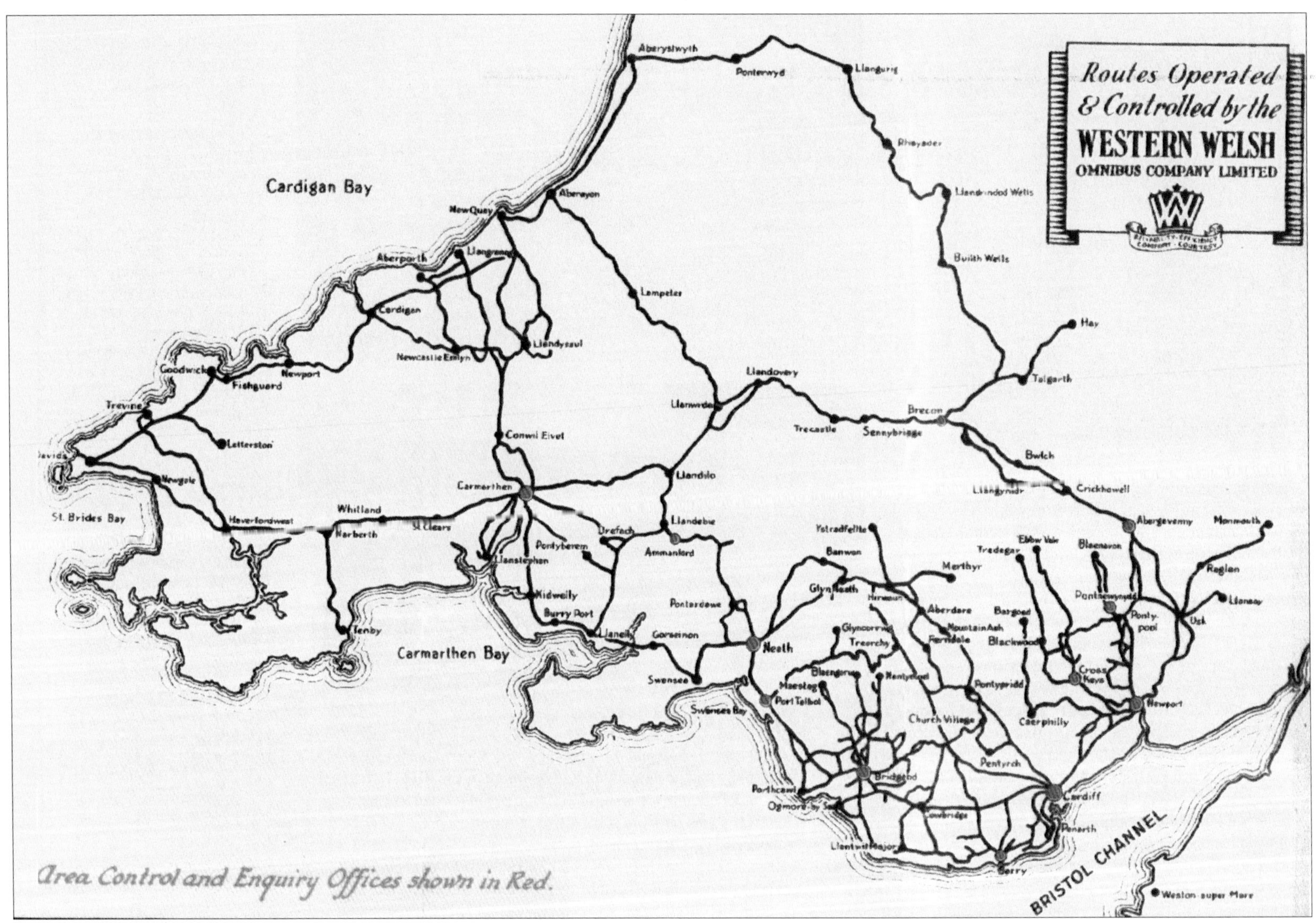

Routes Operated & Controlled by the
WESTERN WELSH
OMNIBUS COMPANY LIMITED
Cardigan Bay
Aberystwyth
Ponterwyd
Llangurig
Rhayader
Llandrindod Wells
Builth Wells
Hay
Talgarth
Aberayron
New Quay
Aberporth
Cardigan
Lampeter
Llandyssul
Newcastle Emlyn
Goodwick
Fishguard
Newport
Trevine
Letterston
Newgale
St. Brides Bay
Haverfordwest
Whitland
Narberth
St Clears
Conwil Elvet
Carmarthen
Llandovery
Llanwrda
Trecastle
Sennybridge
Brecon
Bwlch
Llangynidr
Crickhowell
Llandilo
Llandebie
Drefach
Ammanford
Pontyberem
Llanstephan
Kidwelly
Burry Port
Llanelly
Gorseinon
Pontardawe
Tenby
Carmarthen Bay
Swansea
Swansea Bay
Neath
Ystradfellte
Banwen
Glynneath
Hirwaun
Merthyr
Aberdare
Mountain Ash
Ferndale
Treorchy
Blaengarw
Maesteg
Port Talbot
Pontypridd
Church Village
Caerphilly
Tredegar
Ebbw Vale
Blaenavon
Abergavenny
Monmouth
Raglan
Usk
Pontypool
Blackwood
Bargoed
Cross Keys
Newport
Pentyrch
Bridgend
Porthcawl
Cowbridge
Cardiff
Penarth
Llantwit Major
Barry
BRISTOL CHANNEL
Weston super Mare
Area Control and Enquiry Offices shown in Red.

arrangements with caution, an article about these days in a subsequent Western Welsh *Staff Bulletin* observes that 'huge sighs of relief were heard all around that local authorities were no longer involved in licensing!'. Particularly difficult had been the relationship with Barry Urban District Council, which in 1929 had sought to insist upon two-door buses in its area. Councillor C. B. Griffiths didn't mind that single-door buses were acceptable to Scotland Yard and the Ministry of Transport: 'We don't want them here!' He envisaged a scenario whereby a bus would be hit in the fuel tank, and everyone in front of it would be 'caught like rats in a trap'. When asked how often the scene he so vividly described occurred, he claimed that 'dozens of them were taking place'. Despite assurances that the Council had no powers over bus design, Cllr Griffiths refused to agree!

To a large extent the Act, with its imposition of much bureaucracy, sorted out the short-term players from those who wished to become a more permanent part of the growing industry. Decisions soon became more balanced, and this influenced the fledgling Western Welsh, operator number TGR441 and firmly in the latter camp, in two important ways. Firstly, the promise of stability accelerated building plans, land being bought in Carmarthen, Ammanford and Bridgend in 1930 alone. Secondly, the company actively sought to buy up other operators which it thought would not survive in the new regulated environment. Indeed, the company did rather well out of the Act, gaining the excellent through route from Newport to Bargoed via Caerphilly, but missed out on the Cardiff–Swansea route; this went to Neath & Cardiff Luxury Coaches — a decision that always rankled. Indeed, jointly with South Wales Transport, WW introduced a competing service, but this was unsuccessful and lasted for only a few months; so poorly supported was it that crews would stop at St Nicholas for a cup of tea! This spurred Western Welsh into introducing a limited-stop Cardiff–Port Talbot service that was gradually extended until it became the mighty 74-mile Cardiff–Carmarthen route.

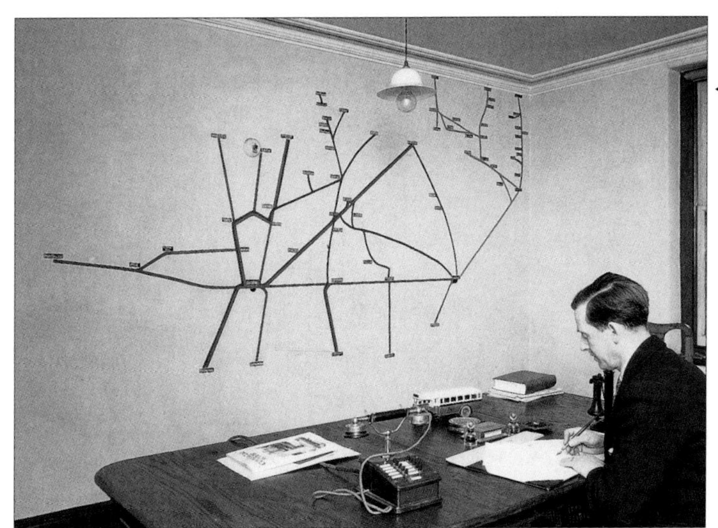

◄◄ The company established control centres throughout its area, as shown on the map opposite.
◄ The interior of one is shown in the accompanying picture.
Viv Corbin collection; Christine Davies collection

▼ Driver's licences issued by Barry and Pontypridd councils to Donald Bell in 1930. Don would later become a much-respected Superintendent at Cardiff bus station, where he worked from its opening until his death in 1967. Starting with SCWM, he was descended from the Bell and Yard families, two stalwarts at Severn Road horse-tram depot in the famous Solly Andrews empire.
courtesy John Reypert

Licence No. 1736

Barry Urban District Council.

Char-a-banc, Hackney Carriage, Wagonette, Brake or Omnibus Driver's or Conductor's Licence.

Badge No. 1138

TO ALL WHOM IT MAY CONCERN.

Be it known by these Presents *that* Donald McMillan B... *residing at* 3 Anglesey Street, Cardiff *is hereby* **Licensed** *to be the* Driver *of an* Omnibus *plying for hire within the Urban District of Barry.*

This Licence to continue in force until the 31st Ma...

unless the same be sooner revoked.

Given under the Seal of the Barry Urban District Council, this fifteenth *of* May 1930

Chairman.

Member.

Clerk.

"Barry & District News," Barry Dock

Licence No. B 247.

HACKNEY CARRIAGE DRIVER'S LICENCE

(MOTOR OMNIBUS).

We, the Urban District Council of Pontypridd, pursuant to the powers and authorities enabling us in this behalf, and upon the application of Donald McMillan Bell residing at 3, Anglesey St, Cardiff do hereby license him to act as a Driver of any Motor Omnibus Hackney Carriage licensed to ply for hire within the Urban District of Pontypridd, subject to the Bye-laws, Rules, Orders and Regulations made or to be made by us under the aforesaid powers and for the time being in force in the said District. This licence commences from the date hereof and will continue in force (unless previously suspended or revoked by us) until the 31st day of December, 1931.

1 JAN 1931

Given under the Common Seal of the Urban District Council of Pontypridd this 16th day of December one thousand nine hundred and 30.

(SEAL.)

Clerk of the Council.

C. K. & Co., Ltd.—14436-1930.

No 140, one of 10 petrol-engined, Park Royal-bodied AEC Regals new in 1930, passes the Royal Tudor Hotel in Cardiff *c*1931. It is on the three-hour run to Ammanford, where passengers could change to reach Llanelly, Carmarthen and, in later years, Aberystwyth. Renumbered 553, this bus would be withdrawn after 10 years and sold to an independent operator. *Viv Corbin collection*

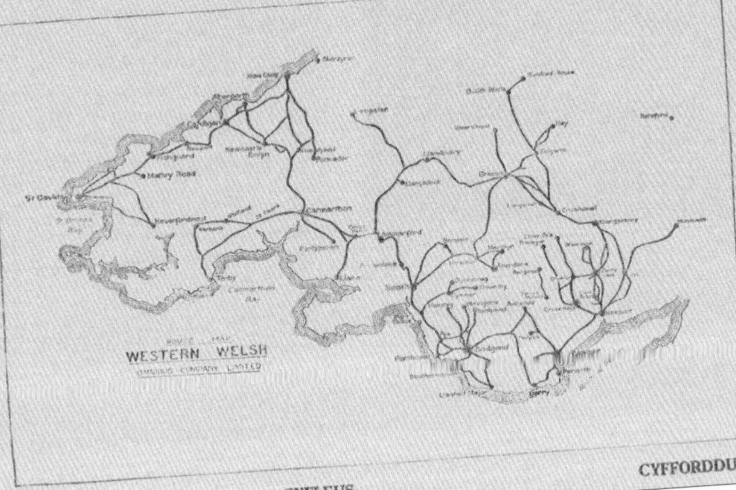

A 1930 Welsh bus map. The top line translates as 'If wishing to see the beauty of the vales and hills of south Wales, travel by bus'; it is old-fashioned Welsh, as 'Deheu' is the older form of 'De', meaning 'South'. The bottom line reads: Cyflym (fast), Cyfleus (convenient) and Cyfforddus (comfortable). It is interesting too that in 1930 the word 'bus' hadn't become a Welsh word, which casts some doubt over the authenticity of today's 'bws' — particularly as Welsh speakers always say 'bus'! *Viv Corbin collection*

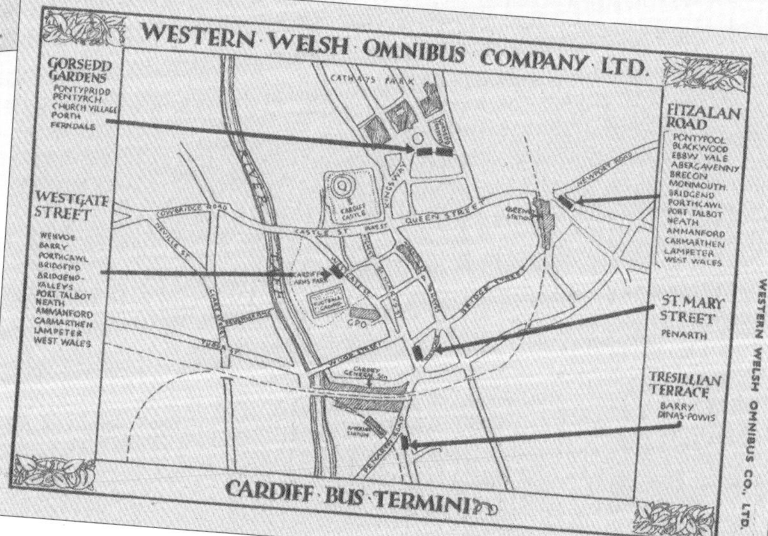

Map showing the termini for WW services within the city of Cardiff. Routes to Bridgend and beyond commenced at Fitzalan Road, just east of Queen Street station; buses employed thereon then called at Westgate Street before leaving the city. Fitzalan Road was also the start point for the company's tours and for services to the eastern valleys. Those entering from the north terminated near Kingsway. This was all not for passengers' benefit but to give some protection to the city's tramways. In the 1940s services to Barry moved from Tresillian Terrace to Raven Street, just off Wood Street. *Viv Corbin collection*

The first company purchase, in 1929, was of Paskin of Brecon, bringing a route from there to Lampeter. This was followed by one-bus operators Edwards Bros and A. Bowen, both of Carmarthen, purchased for £700 and £650 respectively (perhaps the brothers were better negotiators!) in 1930. Griffiths & Davies of Newbridge, with four Thornycroft buses, followed in 1931, while 1933 brought two Porthcawl operators, Morgan Weeks and Francis Motors; no vehicles were included in either deal, these being bought back by their former owners. The latter's purchase price of £2,500 was shared with Rhondda Transport, which stumped up £400 and brought its buses to the town, well outside its traditional operating area but linking the Rhondda coalfields with the popular resort. The first new Western Welsh bus was a Daimler demonstrator, bought in August 1929 but later returned.

On the buildings front, the grand new workshops in Ely were opened in February 1931, having cost £23,800. It was an optimistic time for buses in the city, Cardiff Corporation opening its new premises in Sloper Road five months later. Albert Gray's first son, Leslie, who had joined SWCM in 1919, became Assistant Engineer at the new facility, supporting Chief Engineer Jack H. Lewis, the Western Valleys man. In 1932 new offices were opened in Station Square, Neath, and on 12 April 1933 a fine new bus station, costing £10,493, was commissioned on the site of the old cattle market in Bridgend. In March 1933 WW agreed to pay Cardiff Corporation £100 per annum for the use of a proposed new bus station. It opened 21 years later!

Western Welsh did not immediately master the new rules, and in September 1932 Traffic Manager R. A. J. Williams, an ex-GWR man, was relegated to Area Manager after the Commissioners had revoked some licences due to irregularities. He was replaced by W. T. James, the other ex-Western Valleys man, who went on to become General Manager in 1938 and Managing Director in 1947. Sadly, Managing Director W. B. Cownie, so long associated with the company, died in December 1932, to be replaced early the next year by F. E. Stanley; however, his name was perpetuated by the Cownie Cup, eagerly fought over every year by bus-company teams on the football pitch.

The new company had selected the SWCM livery of red and cream with a brown waistband, but this gradually evolved into just red and cream or yellow, applied in varying styles. However, it seems there remained a strong hankering for the old powder blue and cream of Western Valleys, for some coaches purchased in 1930/1 were delivered in lavender blue and cream. Vehicle policy was based on AEC and Leyland, and in November 1931 the first order was placed for double-deckers — two Leyland Titans and two AEC Regents, at a cost of £1,450 each. In a tidying-up exercise in November 1933 Eastern Valleys and Western Valleys, each with about 40 vehicles of AEC, ADC, Dennis and Thornycroft manufacture, were absorbed by Western Welsh, the companies being wound up. It was more than tidying up; almost £2,000 a year was saved by reducing staff wages to Cardiff and Bridgend levels! Losses of £1,760 for 1929 and £3,004 for 1930 were turned into profits of £12,624 in 1931 and £8,290 in 1932, with a fleet total of 260.

Amongst all this, in January 1931, the controlling NECC group was taken over by BET. NECC continued to hold the shares and control the company, but, portentously, in April 1932 the Head Office was moved to BET's at 88 Kingsway, London.

In July 1933 the company abandoned some of its far-flung routes in the Brecon, Erwood and Llandrindod Wells areas, these being taken up by one Frederick Gwynne Jones, of Erwood Inn. Apparently Mr Jones promised a crate of alcohol in return but died before fulfilling his part of the bargain! Western Welsh just couldn't give up the drink!

▲ Occupying an eight-acre site, the Central Works at Ely, Cardiff, opened in 1931. This early view features an AEC Renown (left) and a number of prewar Leyland Tigers. *Christine Davies collection*

Leaflet for the opening of the new Bridgend bus station in 1933. Albert Gray drew the picture himself. *Christine Davies collection*

Four double-deckers were purchased in November 1931. Albert Gray favoured Leylands, NECC AECs, so two of each were bought — sounds like a reasonable compromise! Nos 171/2 were all-Leyland Titans, 173/4 AEC Regents bodied by Park Royal. The Leyland shown here, 172, went to Western Valleys in January 1933 but returned when that company was absorbed by WW. Regent 174 shows the more simple style of fleet numbers. *Chris Taylor collection*

One of the early double-deckers in the fleet was lowbridge Brush-bodied AEC Regent 175, new in May 1932. Later numbered 252 then 582, it had its petrol engine replaced during the war by a Gardner 6LW diesel. It was withdrawn from Crosskeys in 1949. *Kenneth Evans collection*

▲ New to Eastern Valleys in 1927 as its No 16, this all-Leyland Lion PLSC became WW 19. It had gained the WW crest above the indicator, a distinctive feature in the early days. It was scrapped in 1938. *Chris Taylor collection*

WW letterhead from 1934, showing the registered office as 88 Kingsway. *Chris Taylor collection*

Western Welsh Omnibus Company Ltd.
IN ASSOCIATION WITH GREAT WESTERN RAILWAY.
Directors: J. S. AUSTEN, Chairman; The Rt. Hon. LORD GLANELY, R. COPE, H. C. DRAYTON, Sir JAMES MILNE, F. C. A. COVENTRY, F. E. STANLEY, J. S. WILLS.

Telegraphic Address: "OVERHAULED, LONDON."
Telephone No.: HOLBORN 7888

PRINCIPAL GARAGE: COWBRIDGE ROAD, ELY, CARDIFF.
Telephone and Telegrams: LLANDAFF 327-8.

All Business Communications to be addressed to the Company.

Your Ref. ....
Our Ref. EAB/KM

REGISTERED OFFICE:
88, KINGSWAY,
LONDON, W.C.2.

13th July 1934.

BEF
19 JUL 1934

▲ No 190 (KG 2206) was an all-Leyland LT5 with 35-seat body, new in 1933. The livery now includes the distinctive crest on the side. The bus would later become No 83. *Chris Taylor collection*

◀ This artist's impression was used for publicity purposes in the mid-1930s. Surprisingly the vehicle chosen to lead the line-up was one of the Lion LT5s supplied in 1932 to the associated Western Valleys company. It became WW No 79 in November 1933 before being sold to Alma Queen of Brynmawr in 1949. *Viv Corbin collection*

5. The Early BET Years

In July 1934 Western Welsh became a member of the British Electric Federation Ltd (BEF)[1], a development which manifested itself in the company's adoption of the Federation's standard design of single-deck bus. Early attempts to purchase Green's Motors of Haverfordwest, Pencoed Motors near Bridgend and the buses of Caerphilly UDC failed, but in October £1,850 secured the business of Thomas Bros, along with two buses (five others being retained by Thomas and sold separately) in picturesque Llanstephan, Carmarthenshire. The year ended with the announcement of a profit for 1933 of £13,425.

In comparison with other bus companies Western Welsh was slow to appreciate the benefits of the diesel engine. By the mid-1930s this was becoming more efficient than a comparable petrol engine, while the price advantage of heavy fuel oil — at less than 5d (2p) a gallon some 65% cheaper than motor spirit at 1s 3d (6p) — was enormous. Of course, as soon as anything becomes popular the government will tax it. This happened in 1935, when, to put it on a par with petrol tax, the tax on diesel was raised from 1d to 8d — a 700% increase, making the tax twice the cost of the fuel! However, it still cost 20% less than petrol and gave more miles to the gallon, so there was still a considerable saving to be had. Unfortunately, Western Welsh experienced problems with its first batch of diesels, some 8.8-litre AEC buses bought in 1934, which suffered crankshaft problems in particular. It was much more pleased with the 8.6-litre Leyland engines in a batch of Tiger TS7s bought the next year — so pleased, in fact, that it bought more than 200 of the TS7 and TS8 models before production ceased in 1940. From 1935 onwards all Western Welsh buses bar some Bedfords and a few second-hand purchases were diesel-powered.

[1] It was not until 1943 that BEF changed its name to the BET Federation, following the division the previous year of operating companies jointly owned between it and the Tilling group.

Eight AEC Regal/Weymann saloons delivered in 1934 had the first oil engines in the WW fleet. They cost £1,565 each but were not without their problems, and no more AEC saloons came for 18 years. The seven remaining after the war were rebodied by Burlingham, and this one, 572, lasted until 1952. *David Kershaw collection*

No 104 was a 1935 all-Leyland TS7 with all-metal bodywork that proved none too successful. This photograph shows clearly the crest and fleetname style. This bus was sold to the WD, returning later and being given a second-hand body. *Chris Taylor collection*

◂ A batch of four magnificent petrol-engined AEC Renowns, 185-8, with 56-seat Weymann bodies to a high specification, were delivered in 1933 for limited-stop services. They were painted in Western Valleys lavender blue and cream, Mr Lewis now being Chief Engineer. Unfortunately they were not a success, being extremely heavy on fuel, and the following year they were part-exchanged for diesel-engined Regents. Dealer Romilly Motors then hired them to Thos White, and in due course they came back to WW as 593-6. During the 1930s they were used as little as possible, and 593 was burned out in 1941. The others were included in the wartime re-engining programme with diesels, which greatly reduced their fuel consumption. Postwar they gained bus livery and were upseated to 60. *Chris Taylor collection*

▴ ◂ The four forward-entrance Regents that replaced the Renowns took fleet numbers 257-60, held briefly by the Renowns before their sale. Very similar to London Transport's 'Godstone' STLs, they had 8.8 litre engines and 48-seat Weymann bodies. *Chris Taylor collection*

The year 1935 also saw more takeover activity, some of it unsuccessful. Hughes of Trimsaran and James of Ammanford (later to become a BET company in its own right) declined, and Newport Coporation wouldn't even talk to Western Welsh when the suggestion was made! However, there were some notable successes. F. J. John of Nantyfyllon brought four Thornycroft buses for £11,500 in January, these being followed in June by another nine Tilling-Stevens and AJS buses from W. T. Jones, trading as Express Motors, of Bryncethin. He held out for £15,000.

But by far and away the major expansion was the takeover under a hiring agreement in July 1935 of Thos White & Co of Cardiff and Barry. This brought a network of services in the Cardiff, Barry and Pontypridd areas and a fleet of 72 buses made up of AEC Regals, Regents and three-axle Renowns, Leyland Lions, ADC 416, 417 and 426 types and even a solitary Ramillies. Depots were located in Cardiff and Barry. Some of the routes were in competition with Western Welsh; indeed, the Penarth service was referred to as having the feel of an unofficial Brooklands meeting, for Western Welsh Lions and White's single-deck Renowns could often be seen tearing neck-and-neck up Windsor Road past Penarth Police Station! The purchase allowed rationalisation of these services; indeed, Albert Gray had been working on such plans for a number of years. Equally significant was the Cardiff–Ferndale service via Pontypridd, which took WW buses deep into Rhondda Transport territory. Included in the price of £85,000 was the two-vehicle subsidiary of C. J. Vincent of Cardiff. It is interesting that both White's and Western Welsh had strenuously denied a rumoured takeover of the former in 1930 at a suggested sum of £100,000! Both acquired companies were finally liquidated in December 1936, White's valued at £34,233 and Vincents at £239. Along with White's Western Welsh gained Fred Pengelly. He had started as a conductor in 1926 and upon takeover was appointed as temporary manager at Cardiff and Barry at £400 per annum. By 1952 he was Traffic Manager, becoming Assistant General Manager a year before his retirement in 1972. Fred often appeared on the expanding medium of television, either to put the company's view or to publicise its tours programme. He very much became the public face of Western Welsh and encouraged the purchase of coaches. It is difficult to understand what went wrong with White's. It had a large fleet operating in a growing area, all the right ingredients for success. The founder, Thomas White, who started the business in 1908, had

Tom White's original premises in Broad Street, Barry, *c*1909. *Chris Taylor collection*

The occasion is unknown, but WW really went to town on this private hire to the New Theatre in Greyfriars Road, Cardiff. The year is 1935 and the lead coach was 59, a 1930 Leyland LT2 with Northern Counties body. Originally painted light blue and cream, it was now cream and red. Behind the low building on the left can be seen the remains of Greyfriars House, which would be cleared in 1967 to make way for the Pearl building, then the tallest in Cardiff. *Viv Corbin Collection*

▲ At the Cardiff bus stop in Pontypridd is White's UH 2242, an AEC Renown of 1927 with 32-seat United body. It would pass to WW as a non-runner. *Chris Taylor collection*

▲ During the time that White's was leased by Western Welsh, the vehicles were painted in WW livery instead of blue and cream but with White's fleetnames. Seen at Barry Island is No 91, a Thornycroft AV2 with Smith body. It became WW No 385. *Chris Taylor collection*

One of the magnificent AEC Renowns of White's. It was numbered 100, had a Short Bros lowbridge body and was new in December 1931. Its petrol engine was replaced by a diesel in June 1935, and the bus eventually became WW No 598. *Chris Taylor collection* ▶

The bus terminus in Pontypridd, with a Leyland Tiger at the stop and Pontypridd UDC trolleybus wires in evidence. This was once a tramroad to the Rhondda and was a dead end. It is now a main road.
Chris Taylor collection

begun talks with Western Welsh in 1933 at a time of considerable expansion, but in January 1935 he died. The mists of time obscure, but one can't help feeling that all was not well with the company. Whatever, the acquisition was great news for Western Welsh and put the company in a commanding position in the lucrative Barry market, although the local council wasn't happy — it had liked the competition!

Also in July 1935 J. Jones of Pontyberem and associated companies were bought, (no vehicles changing hands), as was Danygraig Motor Services Ltd of Newport, for £6,000, bringing only one bus, although the company was to remain registered until 1940, Western Welsh buses being drafted in 'on hire'.

Danygraig Omnibus Services, taken over by Western Welsh in 1935, was typical of the acquisitions that helped build up the company. WO 402 is a Thornycroft A1 with Hall Lewis 20-seat body. This bus was not kept by WW; only one was — a Dennis Lancet. The destination is spelt wrongly; there should be an 'E' on the end.
Chris Taylor collection

If all this were not enough, Western Welsh decided that there was an opportunity to launch a programme of extended tours. So for the 1935 season a programme of 12 departures was provided, offering 14 days in the Scottish Highlands, nine days in Edinburgh and the Trossachs, seven days in Devon and Cornwall and a 'Welsh Wonderland' lasting six days. Coaches used were Leyland Tigers with 21 seats of the armchair type, upholstered in green. One-time Tours Manager Ken Allender recalled that in terms of comfort they compared well with modern coaches. For many years after they had finished their time on the road some of these seats were provided for anyone visiting the General Manager or Traffic Manager at Head Office, while some of the material graced Christine Davies' doll's house as carpets! Such was the success of the tours programme that the Lake District, East Anglia and the South Coast were added in 1937, increasing the number of departures to 20. By 1939 tours had become firmly established ('their popularity is ever increasing,' assured the brochure), and 65 departures were offered. However, the war brought a temporary halt to this significant part of the company's business.

Financially things were heading in the right direction, a profit of £26,958 being announced for 1934; this solid progress continued in 1935 with a profit of £45,172. Bert Langley's business in Abersychan was bought in February 1936 for £1,500, while the Cardiff–Aberystwyth express-service licences held by Red & White were acquired for £7,000 in July, along with three buses operated by Gough's Welsh Motors of Mountain Ash; this company had earlier been bought out by Red & White, but an existing agreement with Western Welsh meant that R&W could not operate the services. These, added to WW's own, became the basis for a network of express services throughout the company's area, Aberystwyth remaining the main destination right through to the 1970s. Profits for 1936 increased to £61,874.

The year 1937 brought two more operators into the fold. In January Phipps Motor Services of Glyn Neath brought eight vehicles, including some Thornycrofts, for £15,000, while in April came Green & White Services of Bridgend, strengthening the base there; the £13,025 deal covered a garage and 13 vehicles including Bedfords and Albions. In July Pencoed Motor Co succumbed, bringing some Guys and ex-Devon General Leyland Lions in return for £10,000. Both Green & White and Pencoed remained as limited companies, with WW buses drafted in, until 1938 and 1941 respectively.

◂ One of the four Weymann-bodied Tiger TS7s delivered in 1935 to commence extended tours. It spent some time with the WD before returning to WW as a service bus. *Chris Taylor collection*

▴ One of the 1935 tour coaches stands outside an elegant hotel somewhere on the British mainland; WW did not stray abroad. *Christine Davies collection*

◂ Coaches 209-14, Leyland Tigers with centre-entrance Duple bodywork, line up on a private hire in 1936, the year they were new. No 214 was on hire to White's Motors, as new WW vehicles replaced some of White's older buses that year. Five of these vehicles would receive new Burlingham bus bodies in 1946. *Viv Corbin collection*

▲ The company purchased only six Leyland Cubs — two in 1935 and four in 1936. This is No 216, new in May 1936. These buses were delicensed when war was declared, and some saw war duties with the authorities; 216 was hired to a Royal Ordnance factory, returning to Bridgend in 1946. The following year it became an engineering van at Ely, lasting thus until 1952. *Kenneth Evans collection*

▲ Standing outside the Abergavenny depot of Red & White is 1935 Brush bodied Tiger 133, surrounded by R&W stock. The building was still standing in 2007 but was no longer a bus garage. *Chris Taylor collection*

◄ On 3 August 1953 No 714 has made the steep climb to the top of Maerdy Mountain on the long journey from Aberystwyth. This was a summer-only express working — and how typical of Western Welsh to use a bus such as this, an ECW-bodied Leyland TS8 new in 1939! It would last until 1956, when it passed to a contractor. *Alan Jarvis*

There were only three examples of the Bristol make in the prewar WW fleet. Following a trial in 1936 a pair of JO5Gs were ordered with sliding-roof ECW bodywork. Nos 401 (seen here) and 402 entered service in March 1937. The third, an L5G, was delivered after being exhibited at the 1937 Show. Sharing duties at Bridgend and Port Talbot, they were all withdrawn in March 1954. *Kenneth Evans collection* ▶

An impressive private hire outside the GWR station in Cardiff on 24 July 1937. The notorious and ill-named Temperance Town has been levelled, and 17 years later the new bus station would open on this site. The coaches are a mix of AEC Regal/Northern Counties, Leyland Tiger/Duple, Tiger/Weymann and Lion/ Northern Counties. At the front on the right is the unique TSM/Beadle delivered direct to WW when it took over Jones of Bryncethin. It arrived in WW colours, on the strict understanding that it would be painted into Jones livery if the deal fell through. It became one of the first coaches in the cream-and-red livery. It is pleasing to see this job being covered entirely by coaches in coach livery — an occurrence which, sadly, was all too rare! *Chris Taylor collection* ▼

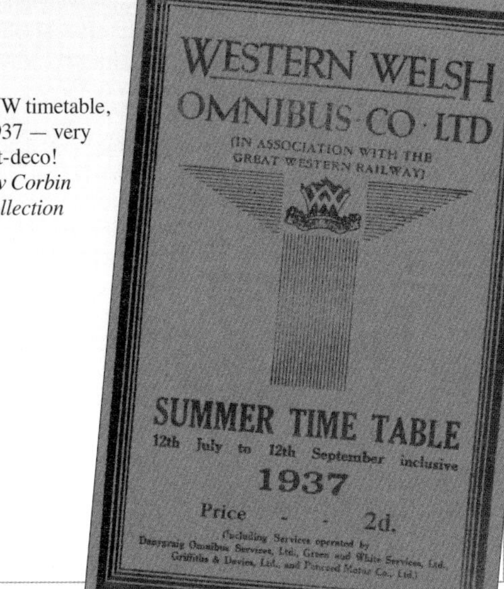

WESTERN WELSH
OMNIBUS CO LTD
(IN ASSOCIATION WITH THE GREAT WESTERN RAILWAY)

SUMMER TIME TABLE
12th July to 12th September inclusive
1937

Price - - 2d.

(Including Services operated by Danygraig Omnibus Services, Ltd., Green and White Services, Ltd., Griffiths & Davies, Ltd., and Pencoed Motor Co., Ltd.)

WW timetable, 1937 — very art-deco! *Viv Corbin collection*

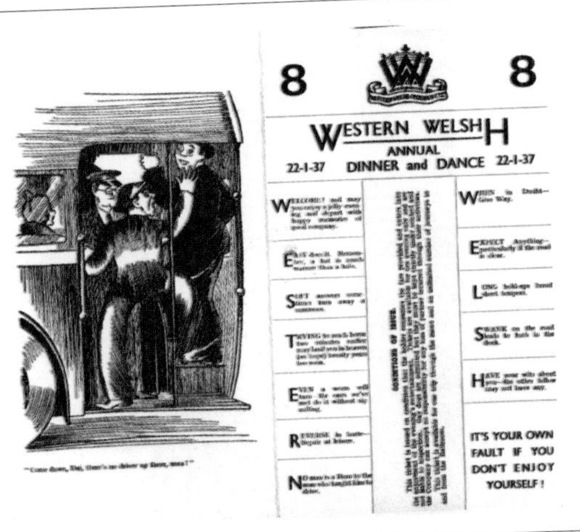
8 8

WESTERN WELSH

ANNUAL

22-1-37 DINNER and DANCE 22-1-37

IT'S YOUR OWN FAULT IF YOU DON'T ENJOY YOURSELF!

Menu card for the 1937 Dinner Dance. *Viv Corbin collection*

Building expansion continued in 1937, the ex-White's depot in Penarth Road, Cardiff, being expanded at a cost of £9,000 following the previous year's purchase of adjoining land for £3,000. The year ended with a joint-working agreement with Cardiff Corporation over the Penarth service (both operators having spent much of the decade trying to reduce the sums paid in tolls for the use of Penarth Road) and the purchase for £11,000 of the Neath–Banwen route from Osborne Services via South Wales Transport. Western Welsh felt it paid too much. Still, things looked set fair, a profit of £73,806 being recorded for the year.

In 1938 there was a concerted effort to become firmly established in Barry. The previous year GWR land had been set aside to build a depot, and in June 1938 it was proposed to increase the size of this to enable the purchase of all competing services in the town. A good start was made the following month with the purchase of the local services and excursion and tours licences of F. L. Harfoot, S. Harfoot & Sons, A. H. Evans, J. Issac and W. J. Knight (although Harfoot's was continue as a major local haulier until 1976). The combined £21,100 price tag for this lot included £800 for the 14 buses, which included more Thornycrofts. Many of the bus routes duplicated Western Welsh services, so, again, rationalisation was possible. Two months later, £9,000 was paid for J. H. Hill of Barry, again bringing bus and coach work; the 11 vehicles included Leyland Lions, again ex-Devon General, and Dennises new to South Wales Transport. Two significant links with the past were severed with the retirement in August of Albert Gray (although he was retained as a consultant at £700 per annum) and the return a month later of the lease on 8/8A Penarth Road to Hancocks.

Western Welsh entered 1939 with a great deal of building work in hand to accommodate the expanding fleet. The new Barry base at Broad Street opened early in the year, costing £13,983 and accommodating no fewer than 52 buses — quite an achievement for a company that had previously washed its hands of the place! A new 19-vehicle depot at Gadlys in Aberdare opened in the summer, while the Pontnewynydd depot near Pontypool was expanded to hold 60 buses. Meanwhile £10,800 was spent on doubling the size of Penarth Road garage in Cardiff, and land was purchased for new depots in Brecon and Crosskeys and for further extensions in Cardiff and Bridgend. Two further takeovers comprised the one-bus (a Thornycroft) Barry route of J. H. Woodfield for £2,000 in January, followed by the £1,250 purchase of two-vehicle J. David & Son of Aberkenfig in April; in both cases the buses themselves were not used. In July Share capital was increased to £600,000; the paid-up shares amounted to 507,500, of which the GWR held 193,750, BET 137,400 and NECC 92,250. During the course of the year it was announced that profit on the company's 487 buses had increased to £88,058 in 1938.

Although the company would end up recording a profit of £97,617 for 1939, Western Welsh's development was halted by the declaration of war on 3 September. Negotiations, jointly with Red & White, for the purchase of Cardiff coach firms Cridlands and Forse ceased, and the realisation that better vehicles were needed for coach work remained just that, as a proposed order for six new coaches of the latest style was not placed.

Dark days lay ahead.

Only three Leyland saloons came in 1938, all TS8s with 35-seat ECW bodywork. No 307 was one of a number of vehicles to feature a mainly white livery for use on limited-stop services. It lasted until 1954 at Ammanford. *Kenneth Evans collection*

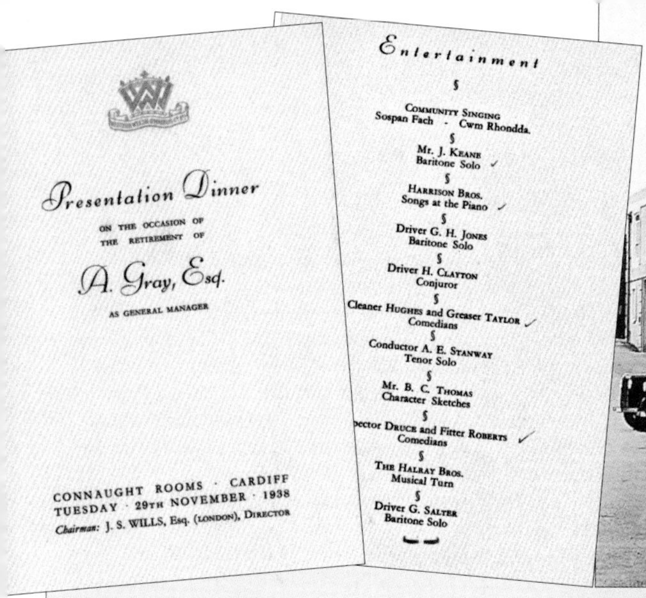

Presentation Dinner

ON THE OCCASION OF THE RETIREMENT OF

A. Gray, Esq.

AS GENERAL MANAGER

CONNAUGHT ROOMS · CARDIFF
TUESDAY · 29TH NOVEMBER · 1938
Chairman: J. S. WILLS, Esq. (LONDON), DIRECTOR

Entertainment

Community Singing
Sospan Fach - Cwm Rhondda.

Mr. J. Keane
Baritone Solo

Harrison Bros.
Songs at the Piano

Driver G. H. Jones
Baritone Solo

Driver H. Clayton
Conjuror

Cleaner Hughes and Greaser Taylor
Comedians

Conductor A. E. Stanway
Tenor Solo

Mr. B. C. Thomas
Character Sketches

pector Druce and Fitter Roberts
Comedians

The Halray Bros.
Musical Turn

Driver G. Salter
Baritone Solo

Menu for the Retirement Presentation to Albert Gray. *Christine Davies collection* ▲

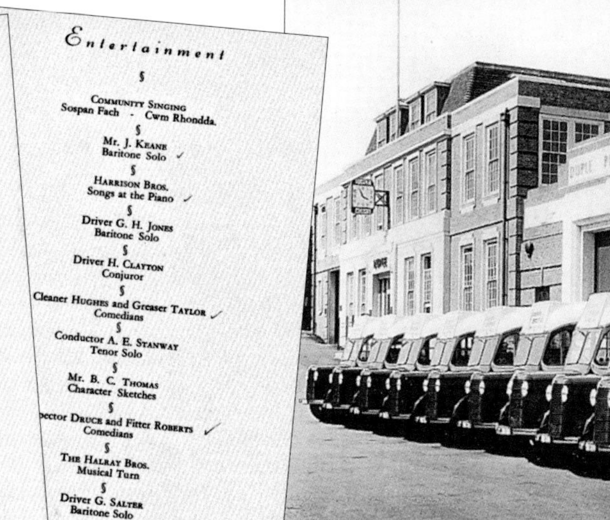

▲ Pictured before delivery from the Duple factory at The Hyde, Hendon, are the 12 Bedford WTBs — Nos 469-80 (BBO 301-12) — supplied in 1938. Featuring a 27hp six-cylinder petrol engine and seating 20, they were chosen as an alternative to the Leyland Cubs purchased in earlier years, probably following the company's experiences with Bedfords taken over from other operators, and lasted until 1950. Nos 478/9 were requisitioned by the military, being bought back late in 1943. *Viv Corbin collection*

◄ Barry Island as we like to remember it, with double-deck buses just keeping up with the loads. In three-cream-band livery, ahead of a 1946 AEC Regent with prewar ECW bodywork (see page 38), is 599, a 1933 Renown with 60-seat Short Bros body. This was a fairly early oil-engined bus, fitted with an 8.8-litre unit. Viv Corbin remembers riding upstairs on it, sitting on one of the long seats on the way to Barry County School one wintry morning in about 1948. Turning from Park Avenue into St Nicholas Road, a steep corner with adverse camber, the driver missed a gear. At once there were screams from almost 90 children as the bus began lurching as it slid towards the edge of a railway embankment. The outcry quickly turned to cheers as the second attempt to climb the hill was successful! *Chris Taylor collection*

WESTERN WELSH
Omnibus Company Limited.

BARRY AREA

REVISED EMERGENCY SERVICES

COMMENCING

SUNDAY, 24th SEPTEMBER, 1939.

and until further notice.

The curtailment of these services has been necessitated by the restriction in the supply of Petrol and Fuel Oil during the National Emergency.

Passengers are assured that every effort will be made to reinstate services when conditions permit.

For details of the Cardiff—Wenvoe—Barry, and Cardiff—Dinas Powis—Barry Services please see Special Bills, obtainable from Conductors or enquiry offices.

W. T. JAMES,
General Manager.

COWBRIDGE ROAD,
ELY, CARDIFF.
September, 1939.

Barry Advertiser T 1474

▲ Wartime reductions, 24 September 1939.
Viv Corbin collection

6. Wartime

It is very difficult for those who have never lived through one to imagine how war takes over in so many ways. In 1939 production turned to the war effort, which for a company like Western Welsh had a number of side-effects. In the first place, factories, army camps and airfields sprang up, all of which required transport, dramatically increasing passenger numbers; even an excursion programme was offered from RAF St Athan! These requirements had built up in the months preceding the outbreak of war, St Athan having previously been something of a rural backwater, and were not without their problems. In January 1939 the company was fined £3 with £2 costs for allowing driver Alcwyn D. Evans to carry 52 people on his 35-seater to St Athan. Alcwyn didn't get away with it either, being fined £2! Known as 'Danny', he was a popular member of the Barry staff, having joined in 1938 from the Issac business.

From 24 September 1939 some services were suspended by the Regional Transport Commissioner, these being mainly rural routes but still accounting for 30% of the company's mileage, but the growth in military and associated traffic meant that overall mileage increased. As an indication, in the Carmarthen area (including West Wales, which saw the largest growth in traffic) the vehicle allocation rose from 30 in 1939 to 63 in 1942, and by 1946 had risen to 89, the increases being entirely due to the growth of Government services. Buses had to be left in the open at such places as Kilgetty, Goodwick, Haverfordwest and Cardigan. Staff volunteered or were called up, or were required for the war effort elsewhere, and skilled engineering staff were soon in very short supply, as were spare parts. With men joining the Armed Forces, many women joined the company as conductors (or 'clippies' as they became known), and their contribution to continuing the service is incalculable. Many stayed on to have long careers with the company. By December 1942, 12 women were being trained as drivers. On top of all this, 18 buses — 12 Leyland Tigers (some of them brand-new), three Cubs, two Bedfords and a TSM — were requisitioned by the Military (some later being bought back), and 29 others were on standby as ambulances for Civil Defence and the Welsh Board of Health. So severe was the situation that a company of the Royal Army Service Corps, along with 60 vehicles, was posted to South Wales to convey war workers. Western Welsh claimed none was used on its routes, but some sources suggest the use of 17 vehicles.

After many years of equipping the fleet with modern vehicles, the supply of new buses dried up. In the years 1941-5 only 25 new buses were delivered, and only three

▶ A batch of Park Royal-bodied Leyland TD7s intended for Southdown of Brighton were distributed, after registration in 1940, to other operators which had had orders cancelled because of the war. WW 776 was one of the seven allocated to the company, the others going to Crosville and Cumberland. It is seen in the less-than-salubrious surroundings of pre-bus-station Wood Street in Cardiff.
Chris Taylor collection

disposed of, all as a result of fires. Double-deckers were borrowed from South Wales; the company was too slow in responding to an offer from East Kent, and finally some Leyland Titans intended for Southdown arrived in October 1940 along with two of the 15 AEC Regents ordered for 1939. Buses scheduled for scrapping had to be kept going when new parts were almost non-existent. Bus stops could not be less than 440 yards apart, to conserve fuel, and a 2d minimum fare was introduced to 'discourage wasteful short riding'! Regulations on standing passengers were relaxed, forward-facing seats were replaced by perimeter seating, while 35-seaters had their capacity increased to over 60! (Bet 'Danny' wasn't amused!) Parts of Crosskeys and Barry depots were requisitioned for military use, meaning all depots had to be camouflaged and (by April 1941) equipped with air-raid shelters. Barry depot was scheduled for use as a mortuary, and, in the early days of the war, when invasion seemed certain, plans were laid to use the buses for mass evacuation. Early in the war all bus roofs were painted grey, and many buses painted grey all-over.

ALL BUSINESS COMMUNICATIONS TO BE ADDRESSED TO THE COMPANY

WESTERN-WELSH OMNIBUS COMPANY LTD

IN ASSOCIATION WITH GREAT WESTERN RLY.

DIRECTORS:
J. S. AUSTEN (Chairman) H. C. DRAYTON
RT. HON. LORD GLANELY SIR JAMES MILNE, K.C.V.O.
SIR RALPH COPE F. E. STANLEY
F. C. A. COVENTRY J. S. WILLS

GENERAL MANAGER: — W. T. JAMES

HEAD OFFICE
COWBRIDGE ROAD,
CARDIFF.

TELEGRAMS LLANDAFF 327
TELEPHONE LLANDAFF 327-8-9
REGISTERED OFFICE: 88, KINGSWAY, LONDON, W. C. 2.
TELEPHONE: HOLBORN 7868

YOUR REF ________ OUR REF SBN/JHH.

OFFICES AND GARAGES

ABERDARE
GADLYS ROAD
TELEPHONE 279

WW letterhead from 1941, showing the company still registered in London but with Cowbridge Road as its Head Office — a wartime measure.
Chris Taylor collection

◂ In 1942 the company was allocated four 'unfrozen' AEC Regents with highbridge utility bodywork by Northern Coachbuilders of Newcastle. They featured the reliable 7.7-litre engine and, with utility Guys delivered later, went some way toward alleviating the wartime shortages. Seen in Cardiff, 607 makes an interesting comparison with lowbridge Regent 637, built eight years later.
Kenneth Evans collection

From December 1942 evening services were drastically cut after 9pm. A side-effect of this was a growth in taxis; in 1939 there were three in Barry, but by 1945 this had risen to 15, and there seems no doubt that some of the wartime measures had a long-term impact on the company and, indeed, the industry as a whole. By this time no less than 30% of mileage was for war workers, and returns on mileage increased to a staggering 21d per mile!

As we have seen, Western Welsh had not been quick to move from petrol to oil engines, but 15 Gardner oil engines were fitted to double-deckers, and the positive impact on fuel consumption was very significant. The engines came from Watts Factors, part of a family involved with Red & White, which must have taken some swallowing!

Despite all the upheavals, prewar building plans continued, the new 45-bus garage at Crosskeys being opened in September 1940, and the 15-bus one at Brecon in January 1941. In January 1944 land was bought for a depot in Ammanford, and in September a six-bus shed was rented in Fishguard. Expansion by acquisition also continued, and, in a deal brokered by Red & White, agreement was reached in November 1943 for the takeover of the five remaining Barry operators, this taking place over the next two months.

In August 1943 General Manager W. T. James, who had replaced Albert Gray, resigned to join BET centrally and was replaced a month later, at an annual salary of £1,200, by Mr R. T. Ebrey. This gentleman had made a name for himself in the bus industry previously at Ribble and East Yorkshire and, affectionately known as R. T. E., soon became a well-known figure at Western Welsh.

Brecon depot, at The Watton, was opened in January 1941 to replace premises inherited from the GWR. It cost £7,406, housed 15 saloons and was a classic piece of WW architecture. The building was sold to a tyre dealer in 1989. *Peter Smith collection*

I AM NO GAS-BAG—

yet it is an event of no small importance that I have been singled out as the first of the Company's fleet to be converted to Gas-producer operation.

Soon you will be seeing me on service towing a small trailer. This generates and provides me with the necessary motive power, thus saving many gallons of petrol, a very important factor these days, particularly as the fuel used is home produced.

Only certain of us have the required qualifications—of which we are very proud—and it is gratifying to know that our period of service will not end with the shortage of petrol supplies.

Some people may be facetious at our expense when they first see the trailer, but we can "take it," because we are doing our share to ease the burden on the greatest transport service of all, the Merchant Navy.

At your service,

Bus 566.

ISSUED BY WESTERN WELSH OMNIBUS Co. LTD.

In October 1942 the Ministry of War Transport instructed the company that 10% of its fleet must be fuelled by producer gas. Only nine units had been ordered, but still the company embraced the idea. The first picture shows the gas trailer, and the second bus 566's explanation! By October 1944 the MWT had abandoned the idea of producer-gas units. *Viv Corbin collection*

Blackout restrictions made driving difficult, and accidents rose: in 1938/9 there had been 1,241, but in 1941/2 there were 1,462 — an increase of 18% in three years. Two people were killed by Western Welsh buses during blackouts in Barry alone. The conductor's job on a darkened bus became well nigh impossible, and assaults on staff by those under the influence of alcohol rose. Crews running into major centres such as Cardiff and Barry could expect to be caught in air raids and had to make the choice between heading for the air-raid shelter or making a run for it! In 1944 Barry Island became subject to an emergency embargo, perhaps as part of D-Day preparations. If all this were not enough, a heavy snowfall in January 1945 caused the collapse of the roof at Bridgend depot, damaging eight buses.

However, in these trying times, the provision of a reliable bus service was seen as a clear indication of a continuation of normality, and Western Welsh staff certainly made an important contribution.

Twelve Bedford OWBs were delivered in 1942/3. The Ministry of War Transport allocated up to 40 of these 32-seat utility bodied buses, but WW decided against a further batch, preferring to wait until diesel buses were available. These were the last petrol-engined buses purchased as new by the company and later had their wooden seats replaced by more comfortable ones. No 493 spent most of its time in Aberdare until withdrawal in December 1951. *Viv Corbin collection*

One of nine utility Guy Arab double-deckers delivered during the war, 370 is seen in drab postwar surroundings in Cardiff, where all these buses spent their working lives. It had a highbridge Park Royal body and was one of the second batch, new in February 1945. The war brought Guy back into building big buses after several years making smaller ones. These examples had Gardner 6LW engines and featured unusual gear positions that sometimes caught out drivers. Having each covered more than 400,000 miles these loyal servants were withdrawn in 1956. *Kenneth Evans collection*

In November 1939 WW ordered a batch of 15 Regents with ECW bodies for delivery by August Bank Holiday 1940. The low-height buses were to take priority, and indeed two were received that year. However, in May 1940 ECW moved from its vulnerable site in Lowestoft to premises at Irthlingborough in Northamptonshire, which were not high enough to accommodate highbridge buses. ECW therefore sent the parts for the remaining 13 bodies to WW, which stored them for six years at Ely. One of the two 1940 deliveries, 602, absolutely captures wartime austerity in its overall grey livery, masked headlights and white-edged mudguards. Note the soldier in full kit about to board. *Chris Taylor collection*

In 1946 all the bits were somehow got together to be mounted on postwar Regent II chassis, the combination of prewar bodywork on such chassis giving an odd appearance. The wood in the bodies having been seasoned for so long, they were solid buses that did not suffer from the rotting problems usually associated with buses of this period. Numbered 608-20 and allocated to Barry, Crosskeys, Cardiff and Bridgend, the postwar deliveries were a mix of lowbridge, represented by 613 in Cardiff, and highbridge, like 611 amongst the washing in Bridgend depot. By 1955 they were estimated to have covered 530,000 miles each. *Viv Corbin; Peter Smith collection*

The hourly picturesque 24-mile service from Newport via Usk to Monmouth was joint with Red & White and was inherited from the GWR. Young 'clippies' from Crosskeys pose with their driver at Monnow Street, Monmouth, not long after the war. Their bus is 728, a 1940 Leyland TS8 with ECW body that was rebuilt postwar by Burlingham; it would serve the company until 1954. In 1955 WW would exchange its share of this service for R&W's section of the Cardiff–Barry route. *Viv Corbin collection*

The most popular bus with travellers in the Barry and Bridgend areas in the years following World War 2 was No 757, an ECW-bodied Leyland TS8. One of six commandeered by the military when brand-new in 1940, it had this cartoon applied during a spell with the US Army. In 1946, when the bus was returned to WW and repainted, the decision was taken to keep the cartoon to recognise the wartime service of the company's buses. Following withdrawal of the 'Ruptured Duck', a ceremony was held at Cardiff City Hall in July 1957 when a framed picture of the bus was presented to the American Consul. The famous panel was then removed from the bus and stored at Ely Works for many years until, like so much, it was thrown out for scrap. That was the end of the 'Ruptured Duck'. Quack! *Viv Corbin collection*

At Rogerstone Aluminium Works a battered WW Tiger, No 132, reveals this to be an early postwar scene. No doubt as a result of the impact on fuel consumption, the crest has been moved to be beside the destination boxes. Even more battered are the three Howells & Withers buses, the Regal on the far right being ex WW. Is the sergeant marching those chaps.
Chris Taylor collection

New in 1937 with an ECW body, Leyland TS8 No 282 received this Burlingham body postwar and survived at Bridgend until July 1956. It is seen about to leave Fitzalan Place in Cardiff on the thrice-daily service to the picturesque Vale of Glamorgan village of Llysworney, with some additional information chalked on the indicator! This route was later extended to Llandow.
Kenneth Evans collection

7. Recovery

Western Welsh emerged from the war years much as all bus companies did: with a worn-out fleet, very few new buses and many that were well past their sell-by date. After so many years of austerity and restrictions, understandably, people wanted to travel again. Western Welsh, providing services to a number of popular leisure destinations, soon found that its problems were being compounded by rapidly increasing demand. Every company was clamouring for new buses, and a stopgap measure was to rebody older chassis. In September 1945 authority was given for 50 (later increased to 60) prewar Tigers to go to H. V. Burlingham of Blackpool for rebodying, and in December the first order was placed for postwar buses — 18 Leyland Tigers, at £2,500 each. In June 1947 the design improvements in oil-engined buses led to a recommended 12-year vehicle life. This is interesting, as Western Welsh had been late to realise the benefits of oil engines, did not embark on a massive re-engining programme and even converted oil-engined Leyland Cubs to petrol! Whether it was the low level of wartime deliveries or particularly persuasive arguments, the 18 Tigers became the first of a fleet of 122 such buses, with 32- or 35-seat bodywork by ECW, Weymann or Willowbrook, that took to the road between 1947 and 1949 and were soon to be found throughout the company's area. Not only were they late in delivery (particularly from Weymann); they were also soon found to suffer from body rot as a result of hastily using unseasoned wood, and many of the Willowbrook-bodied buses were rebuilt by the Bristol firm of Longwell Green. The Weymann bodies also suffered from low windscreens, requiring drivers to bend down to see out! Rebuilding by a number of firms, body swaps and work by Western Welsh itself made this a truly bewildering period! It was the more frustrating as older bodies removed were sold to other operators, which then had many years of trouble-free service from them! Fifteen prewar Leyland Lions were hired in 1945 and then purchased from Ribble of Preston, a similar deal being done over nine Tiger TS7s from Yorkshire Woollen of Dewsbury in 1948, the buses lasting until the early 1950s.

Not so standard were 38 Willowbrook-bodied Crossley saloons that came along in November and December 1949 (Leyland being unable to cope with any more orders) and were shared between Crosskeys, Bridgend and Pontypool. They were not popular, being non-standard and, reputedly, difficult to drive. Maybe they were just different. Some became 'swingers' — buses allocated to Central Works to cover for buses under overhaul, a move not generally welcomed! Nevertheless, by March 1955 they had covered 6,840,000 miles between them and in the end some managed decent lives of between 10 and 12 years, a few latterly being fitted with engines from Leyland TS8s. With all these new buses and 60 rebodies, and with many of the displaced bodies being used in a complex programme to update earlier chassis, Western Welsh seemed set fair and perhaps better placed than many. But there was still a huge backlog to deal with. Added to which there were rumblings from Government about nationalisation, and Western Welsh, along with the rest of BET, lobbied strongly against it.

Another course of action on the vehicle front was to deploy double-deck buses. There was a problem with this. The company's area was criss-crossed by railways that had been built by numerous companies to move coal from the coalfields to the ports. Low bridges abounded, and as a consequence double-decks had not featured much. Although some of the first postwar delivery of AEC Regents with ECW and Brush bodies (and Guys delivered in wartime) were to highbridge specification their use was restricted to the Cardiff and Barry areas, and further deliveries stuck to the lowbridge layout, which even then

▲ Eighty new Leyland PS1 saloons arrived in 1946/7 to relieve the postwar bus shortage. Fitted with the 7.4-litre E181 engine that was developed for a wartime tank, they demonstrated a noticeable drop in performance compared with the 8.6-litre prewar TS8. The 'CUH'-registered batch were fitted with 35-seat rear-entrance ECW bodywork featuring small sliding windows in lieu of the half-drop variety used on earlier saloons; when rubber-mounted these made the interior much quieter. No 827, allocated to Crosskeys, is seen on a private hire in typical 'Valleys' surroundings.
Kenneth Evans collection

▲ Representing the postwar Willowbrook-bodied PS2s is 900, outside the premises of Porthcawl Omnibus in that town. *Viv Corbin collection*

▲ An example of the postwar Weymann design on Tiger 782. Although not obvious from this picture, the windscreen was so low that drivers had to bend over to see out! *Viv Corbin collection*

▲ No 930, seen in Newport, was one of the unpopular Crossleys. They came along as Leyland couldn't supply more than 24 buses out of an order for 62. Many of these buses would be withdrawn early with relatively low mileage and stored at depots, most being sold in 1961. Quite aggressive-looking things! *Kenneth Evans collection*

WESTERN WELSH
OMNIBUS COMPANY LIMITED
(... with the British Electric Traction Co. Ltd., and British Railways)

New Quay & Llangranog

WINTER SERVICE

Commencing Tuesday, 28th September, 1948

TUESDAYS, THURSDAYS and SATURDAYS ONLY

		am	pm			
NEW QUAY (Commercial Hotel)	dep.	9 40	5 20	..	..	..
Maenygroes	,,	9 45	5 25	..	..	..
Nanternis (Chapel)	,,	9 52	5 32	..	..	..
Llwyndafydd (Post Office)	,,	9 55	5 35	..	..	..
Penybont	,,	9 59	5 39	..	..	..
Blaencelyn (Post Office)	,,	10 01	5 41	..	..	..
Capel-Y-Wig	,,	10 03	5 43	..	..	..
Pant	,,	10 08	5 48	..	..	..
Pontgarreg	,,	..	5 52	..	..	..
Pant	,,	..	5 56	..	..	..
LLANGRANOG	arr.	10 12	6 00	..	..	..
		am	pm			
LLANGRANOG	dep.	10 20	6 00	..	..	..
Pant	,,	10 24	6 04	..	..	..
Pontgarreg	,,	10 28	6 08	..	..	..
Pant	,,	10 32	6 12	..	..	..
Capel-y-Wig	,,	10 37	6 17	..	..	..
Blaencelyn (Post Office)	,,	10 39	6 19	..	..	..
Penybont	,,	10 41	6 21	..	..	..
Llwyndafydd (Post Office)	,,	10 45	6 25	..	..	..
Nanternis (Chapel)	,,	10 48	6 28	..	..	..
Maenygroes	,,	10 55	6 35	..	..	..
NEW QUAY (Commercial Hotel)	arr.	11 00	6 40	..	..	..

Issued subject to the Regulations and Conditions published in the Company's Time-Tables, Bills and Notices. Such Regulations and Conditions may be inspected free of charge at any of the Company's Offices.

HEAD OFFICE—
ELY, CARDIFF.
September, *1948*.

REGD. T. EBREY,
General Manager.

—T.2641.—
D. Brown and Sons, Ltd., *Printers*, Cowbridge.

WW timetable, 1948. *Viv Corbin collection*

sometimes fell foul of bridges! With sunken side gangway and four-abreast seating upstairs, they were also uncomfortable and were difficult for conductors to work, and their design restricted them to a lower capacity. Nevertheless, they still offered a useful increase over single-deckers, and 34 all-Leyland PD2s to this layout entered service in 1949/50, 24 being the first into service to the newly authorised 8ft width. They were introduced on the service from Cardiff to Neath and were apparently welcomed by passengers because of the extra width, but more of this anon! They were followed later in 1950 by 24 splendid Weymann-bodied AEC Regent IIIs costing £3,876 each, which were obviously viewed with some pride. However, the introduction of double-deckers was not without its problems. General Manager R. T. Ebrey dropped in on the Neath depot children's party early in 1951 and found himself confronted by driver Eynon Williams, who claimed that the company's prestige had been lowered by the introduction of double-decks in place of the coaches used previously on the 74-mile limited-stop Cardiff– Carmarthen service. He felt that the company was losing money as a result. Mr Ebrey pointed out that with rapidly and constantly increasing costs, including fuel tax and wage increases, it was vital to reduce mileage. The double-decks had removed expensive duplication on this and other services, but he nevertheless took on board Driver Williams's point. In the *Staff Bulletin* of the same month he was able to announce that six new double-decks had been ordered for this service with semi-luxury seating, heaters on both decks, full-length luggage racks and platform doors (though he didn't explain why, after 48 of the new 8ft width, these buses reverted to 7ft 6in!). Three earlier models were also fitted with these refinements as back-up.

Coaches did not fare as well, and the re-equipping by some smaller operators was the cause of some envious comment amongst staff. Indeed, at an Area Managers' meeting instructions were given that the

◂ The 12 AEC Regent III/Brush 56-seaters of 1948 were the first WW Regents to have the bigger (9.6-litre) engine. No 628 is seen in Sardis Road, Pontypridd, in June 1952. Its orange triangle denotes allocation to Cardiff, where it was to spend its entire 12-year life. *Viv Corbin collection*

◂ Gradually the amount of cream relief was reduced until it disappeared altogether, and buses were all-over red. Withdrawn in 'The Field' at Ely, No 951, an all-Leyland PD2 of 1950, is in the previous style, with just one band. It had also received some refurbishment, as evidenced by the alternate rubber-mounted windows. Alan Roberts remembers these buses with fondness: 'I liked the fronts — they had nice faces, as my wife would say.' He caused mayhem climbing into the upper deck with its four-abreast seating arrangement clutching his school cello minus case: 'the spike was a great source of annoyance to everyone.' On one school journey someone dropped a stink bomb on the upper deck: 'Can you imagine 20 screaming schoolkids trying to escape the pungent odour, scrambling over those seats to get to the narrow staircase? I'm sure the driver must have thought the suspension had collapsed.' *Arnold Richardson / Photobus*

word 'coach' was not to be used when quoting for private hires. Nevertheless, coach holidays were reintroduced from 1947 to the Lake District, the South Coast and Isle of Wight, the Trossachs and Welsh Wonderland. Prewar Leyland Tiger saloons were reconditioned and reupholstered and painted in the company's coach livery of red and royal ivory. They were down-seated to 24, space being left at the rear for luggage. A great deal of planning went into the detail of the tours to ensure 'first-class accommodation' for clients. Single rooms allotted by hoteliers were in short supply, and the company made 'every effort to persuade friends (of the same sex) travelling together to share twin-bedded rooms'! And you were thinking it was just running coaches. However, the company unashamedly declared that renewal of its 'bread and butter' bus fleet had to take priority. 'Let us endeavour', it urged its staff, 'to give our patrons the best service we have to offer in every respect.' Although it had 12 striking full-fronted Windover-bodied AEC Regal III luxury coaches ready to go on the road the day 8ft-wide vehicles were permitted in 1950 (and took 12 Regal III/Duple coaches second-hand from Devon General in 1952) Western Welsh gained a reputation for using service saloons on inappropriate duties. A private hire to Carmarthen power station operated by five prewar Tigers resulted in the client's never using the company again.

Seen in Cardiff, 633 was the first of a batch of 24 AEC Regent IIIs, with sleek, rounded, 8ft-wide lowbridge Weymann bodies, that arrived in October 1950. Although still causing conductors difficulty, they were popular with drivers, and some lasted a lengthy 13 years in service. A young Roger Davies was kept amused by the fact that various members of the batch gradually had differing amounts of lower yellow band applied around the bonnet and cab front! *Kenneth Evans collection*

In the light of all this activity it is useful to look at the fleet as it stood at 1 November 1950. Of 504 single-deckers 172 were postwar, while 60 of the prewar vehicles had been rebodied postwar, and 47 deliveries of 1939/40 were non-utility; only eight were utility, these being the remaining petrol-engined Bedford OWBs. Of 106 double-deckers no fewer than 83 were postwar, and a further nine non-utility 1940 deliveries. Thus no fewer than 255 vehicles (or 41.81% of the fleet of 610) had been delivered postwar, giving an average age of 8½ years. Nevertheless, the company was continuing to pursue an extensive scrapping programme to keep pace. However, things always seem to happen to rock the boat, and soon they would.

The buildings side had not been neglected, and in December 1948 a new £8,000 garage opened at Ammanford, to be followed on 25 April 1949 by an eight-bus site at Newcastle Emlyn, costing £7,540. The latter replaced a tin shed in Cawdor Road, reputed to have 'associations with damp and rats', no pit space and insufficient space to swing the proverbial cat'. The fine new garage — 'surely a model of its kind' — was opened with due ceremony by the Chairman of the Urban District Council, and the whole event was regarded as a family party. The day was rounded off by 'an excellent dinner with all the trimmings' provided by the company for all staff at the depot, their duties being covered by Carmarthen staff — an act described by R. T. E. as 'a real example of inter-depot friendship'. Carmarthen staff came off-duty in time to hear songs provided by Driver Davies and witness the General Manager being presented with a silver key by depot staff in thanks. Wonder what happened to it.

There was much social activity covering sports and interests, and the newly formed 'Educational Club' was designed to broaden employees' appreciation of Wales. It soon outgrew that, and in the course of many trips around the UK formed a strong bond with the Sporvejenes Engelsk Club of the Copenhagen transport company. By September 1949 the Educational Club had arranged for the Danes a seven-day tour of South Wales, taking in visits to Western Welsh depots in Cardiff, Crosskeys and Carmarthen, receptions with the mayors of Cardiff, Barry, Neath and Carmarthen, numerous lunches, visits to St Fagans and

No 977 was one of the six semi-luxury all-Leyland PD2/1s delivered in 1951 for the 74-mile Cardiff–Carmarthen service. Crew changes on this service took place at the Head Office in Cowbridge Road: a replacement crew was sent out from Cardiff to take the bus into the city and then bring it back whilst the original crew took their meal break. *Chris Taylor collection*

Internal memo about new Leyland PD2 No 957 .

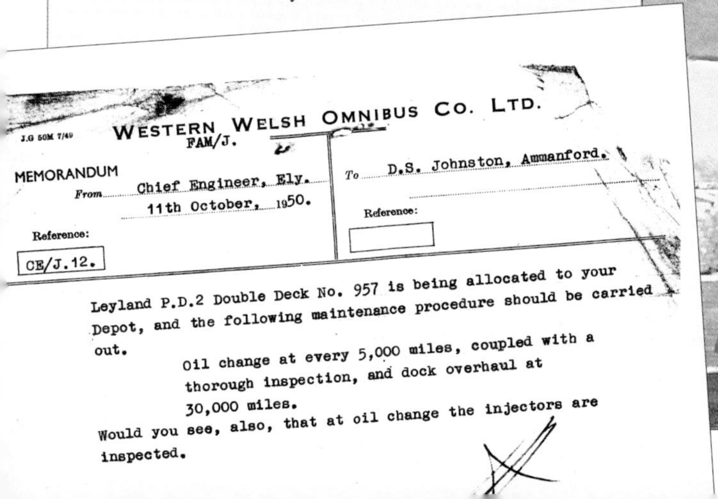

J.G 50M 7/49

WESTERN WELSH OMNIBUS CO. LTD.

FAM/J.

MEMORANDUM

From Chief Engineer, Ely.

11th October, 1950.

To D.S. Johnston, Ammanford.

Reference: CE/J.12.

Reference:

Leyland P.D.2 Double Deck No. 957 is being allocated to your Depot, and the following maintenance procedure should be carried out.

Oil change at every 5,000 miles, coupled with a thorough inspection, and dock overhaul at 30,000 miles.

Would you see, also, that at oil change the injectors are inspected.

No 968, one of the three 1950 PD2/3s subsequently upgraded as back-up for the six buses on the Carmarthen route, shows off its platform doors as it barrels into Milford Haven. *Colin Scott*

◀ EUH 500 was the first postwar coach for WW. It cost £3,644 and was one of 12 AEC Regal IIIs with full-fronted 28-seat coachwork by Windover of Hendon. They entered service the day that 8ft-wide vehicles were legalised. This picture shows the sumptuous surroundings provided for tour passengers. *Viv Corbin collection*

▼ The exterior of sister 508 parked in Oxford. The Regal IIIs later gained extra seats and were painted red and cream, lasting in this form until 1963. *Viv Corbin collection*

Danish visitors at Penarth Road. The Secretary of the Educational Club, Stan Self, received a BEM in 1976 for 'furthering the interests of busmen in both South Wales and Denmark'. *Christine Davies collection* ▶

Cardiff castles, Llandarcy oil refinery, Carmarthen creamery, Taff Merthyr colliery and Welsh Metal Industries' bus plant, tours of coastline and mountains, evenings in social clubs and finally rugby at Cardiff Arms Park! AEC even provided a Monocoach demonstrator to take them back to London. Wow! It was the start of a long and fruitful association between the two operators and shows just what the name 'Western Welsh' could achieve! At the end of the visit the guests presented their hosts with a bronze model of a Viking ship. The gesture was not forgotten, and six years later a model Tiger Cub built at Ely by Coachbuilder W. G. Thomas and painted in fleet colours by Norman Harley (and packed in a realistic crate marked 'another Leyland for export') returned the favour. It was presented by two Cardiff-based staff holidaying with their wives in Denmark. One of the key organisers of these visits was driver Aubigne, the son of a former Barry bus operator.

In August 1947 there had appeared the first issue of the Western Welsh *Staff Bulletin*. Intended as bi-monthly or quarterly, it soon settled down to monthly and from 1951 until 1972 was edited by Stewart Williams of the Publicity Department. Very soon it was reporting the fortunes of depot sports teams, covering all manner of events — including, of course, in South Wales, skittles — as well as births, marriages and deaths, interests and information about the company, social activities, dances (in the Cardiff area held in the legendary Bindles Ballroom at Cold Knap), long-service dinners and safe-driving awards. Also reported were children's Christmas parties, held throughout the patch, and the Educational Club's Field Day behind Ely Works, which was not to be missed. Christine Davies recalls that 'here we would wear fancy dress, run races, watch Punch & Judy, play on swings and a helter-skelter and eat too much ice cream.' The Christmas edition included seasonal tales; in 1966 this included one about a phantom London bus, illustrated with a passable drawing of a Routemaster! Regular reports were received from Copenhagen. Retirements were also noted, and a significant one in September 1950 was that of Brecon leading driver Bill Rhodes, who had joined the GWR in 1889! The *Bulletin* was headed by a message from the General Manager covering all aspects of the company's activities and gave traffic reports and operational statistics — including oil consumption, depot-by-depot, on a monthly basis! In his time R. T. E. pulled no punches. For example, after a strike in West Wales over August Bank Holiday 1949 he appealed in his note: 'Let's apply a little horse sense.' He then itemised the effects on everyone, concluding that these were 'all dead losses to Staff, Public and Company without any compensating gains. Just plain daft!' The *Bulletin* also had a section on public relations, featuring letters received from passengers. All in all it engendered a feeling of belonging, something no doubt much appreciated by staff in the more remote parts of the company. It was to run for 259 issues until crushed by the corporate blandness of the National Bus Company's newspaper-style *Bus* in 1972.

Now you may have noticed that, with all the takeover activity prewar, there has been little mention of the large Red & White company based at nearby Chepstow. Truth is there was an agreement to keep out of each other's patch. Back in the 1930s Western Welsh had also tried to form an agreement with Swansea-based South Wales Transport over jointly taking over smaller operators, but there appears to have been too much suspicion between them, and a number of the targeted companies became BET units in their own right. However, no agreement was made by Red & White with SWT in the Swansea area, and, such was R&W's buying spree there that it set up a whole company, United Welsh, in 1938 to amalgamate its purchases. It got a toehold in Cardiff by resurrecting Liberty Motors (a company it bought in 1936) to get excursion and tour licences in the city and via various associated companies finally came to own Reliance of Barry. The bosses at independent Red & White were canny businessmen, able to move quickly without reference to remote Boards. However, there was a deal of consternation in the camp in October 1947, when, in the heart of the WW/R&W Eastern Valleys area, Jones of Aberbeeg was granted an Ebbw Vale–Newport licence on the basis of the larger operators' not having sufficient buses — a fact blamed squarely by Western Welsh's General Manager on the export drive.

As an indication of the scale of things at this time, a day's takings, reported stolen from Penarth Road garage in Cardiff in April 1948, amounted to £760. In 1950 the company carried 90 million passengers. All its efforts seemed to pay off, a profit of £32,658 for 1944/5 growing to one of £214,191 for 1949/50. Unbeknownst to all at the time, during the period of our tale this was as good as things were to get.

▲ Long Service award.
Viv Corbin collection

▼ A remarkable letter from September 1950, printed as received in the *Staff Bulletin*.

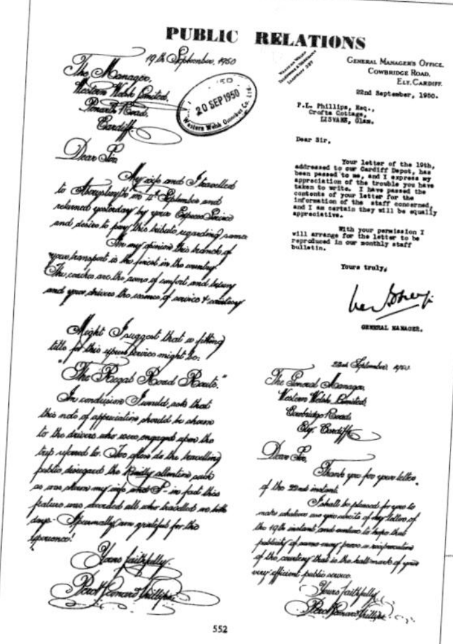

PUBLIC RELATIONS

19th September, 1950

The Manager,
Western Welsh Limited,
Penarth Road,
Cardiff.

20 SEP 1950

Dear Sir,

My wife and I travelled to Aberystwyth on 4th September and returned yesterday by your Express Service and desire to pay this tribute regarding same.

In my opinion this branch of your transport is the finest in the country. The coaches are the acme of comfort and luxury and your drivers the essence of service & courtesy.

Might I suggest that a fitting title for this splendid service might be:
"The Royal Road Route."

In conclusion I would ask that this note of appreciation should be shown to the drivers who were engaged upon the trip referred to. Too often do the travelling public disregard the kindly attention such as was shown my wife and I - in fact this feature was accorded all other travellers on both days. Personally am grateful for the experience!

Yours faithfully,
Percy Leonard Phillips

General Manager's Office,
Cowbridge Road,
Ely, Cardiff.

22nd September, 1950.

P.L. Phillips, Esq.,
Crofts Cottage,
LISVANE, Glam.

Dear Sir,

Your letter of the 19th, addressed to our Cardiff Depot, has been passed to me, and I express my appreciation of the trouble you have taken to write. I have passed the contents of your letter for the information of the staff concerned, and I am certain they will be equally appreciative.

With your permission I will arrange for the letter to be reproduced in our monthly staff bulletin.

Yours truly,

GENERAL MANAGER.

22nd September 1950

The General Manager,
Western Welsh Limited,
Cowbridge Road,
Ely, Cardiff.

Dear Sir,

Thank you for your letter of the 22nd instant.

I shall be pleased for you to make whatever use you desire of my letter of the 19th instant and venture to hope that publicity of same may prove a reciprocation of the courtesy that is the hallmark of your very efficient public service.

Yours faithfully,
Percy Leonard Phillips

552

▸ Tiger Cub 1483 in Penarth.

◂ More delights of Penarth.

▾ A Tiger Cub crosses the river Usk in Brecon.

An Atlantean passes through Aberthaw.

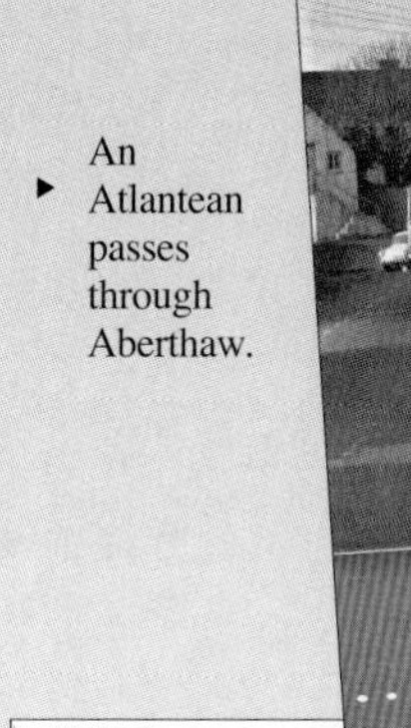

Tiger Cub 1496 makes its way through Cog on its way from Cardiff to the remarkably named Bendricks.

Mothballing coaches with polythene sheets for the winter.

"ON THE ROUTE"

IN his untiring efforts to expand services, the late Mr. Tom White of Barry joined forces with the Rhondda Tramways Co. (as they were then known) and opened up a service between Cardiff—Pontypridd—Ferndale in August, 1930. Five years later his interest in the service was taken over by Western Welsh following the absorption of White's Motors.

Today it is operated with double deck vehicles (eight by W.W. and six by R.T.C., including Cardiff-Pontypridd journeys) at half-hourly intervals between Ferndale and Cardiff with one journey per hour extended beyond Ferndale to Maerdy. The journey time is one hour, twenty minutes ; the route mileage 21.

Leaving Cardiff by way of the Merthyr Road we pass through Taffs Well with Castell Coch perched high in woodland to the right. Castell Coch successfully reproduces the appearance of a type of 13th century Welsh castle of which no authentic example survives intact, and its interior is a particularly striking example of Victorian imaginative decoration. It is in many ways a gigantic sham, a costly folly erected less than 100 years ago by an eccentric Victorian architect to satisfy the antiquarian yearnings of a wealthy nobleman. Yet it has been thought worthy to be taken over and preserved by the Ministry of Works.

Next we reach Nantgarw famed for its porcelain manufactured there by William Billingsley and Samuel Walker in 1813. Their pottery was later transferred to Swansea and many of their beautiful products were decorated by local artists, among them Thomas Pardoe. The name of Nantgarw is world renowned and a large collection of this china can be seen in the National Museum of Wales.

CARDIFF — PONTYPRIDD
SERVICE 330
PORTH — FERNDALE

To-day, the Nantgarw Coke Ovens and By-Product Plant bring further fame to this village. This plant was the first in the country to be erected and completed by the National Coal Board on an entirely new site. The approaches are lined with lawns and flower beds and there are green verges to the two main avenues of the plant. The green hills of the Vale of Taff form a panoramic background against which the reinforced concrete coal bunker, 180 ft. high, the steeply tilted roof conveyors and the soaring stacks form a graceful architectural composition and a good example of modern industrial planning.

Work on the construction of Treforest Industrial Estate began at the end of 1936, and the first factories were occupied in mid-1937. At the present time there are 70 factories producing articles as varied as zipp fasteners, gloves, butterscotch,carbon paper, metal alloys,roller skates,hairdressing equipment, abrasives, flexible tubes,watch straps,mineral waters, dry ice, silk shawls, music strings and artificial flowers.

Pontypridd stands midway between Cardiff and Merthyr Tydfil and is the natural outlet of the Rhondda and Aberdare Valleys. The town derives its name from the remarkable single-span bridge built by William Edwards in 1755. At first unable to solve the problem of the weight involved in the span, Edwards ingeniously inserted three large cylindrical apertures at each abutment, thus lightening the inward and upward thrust. He also succeeded in creating a bridge of great beauty—described as "the beau ideal of architectural elegancy".

Pontypridd has never been entirely dependent upon the local collieries. The chainworks, for example, is an old-established concern. Built on the banks of the old Glamorgan Canal, the works supplied the chain used to moor the ships which fought at Trafalgar. To-day the firm produces single links weighing as much as five hundredweight.

Porth is the gateway to the Rhondda Valleys (Fach and Fawr) ; it is also the home of the Rhondda Transport Company whose offices and workshops are situated in the middle of the town.

The remainder of the journey passes through the closely-knit coal mining communities of Pontygwaith and Tylorstown in the Rhondda-fach to Ferndale. It is difficult to believe that this now populous area was, at the beginning of the 20th century, simply farmland with a few scattered houses. Nowadays a not inconsiderable section of the local community travels daily to Cardiff, resulting in this service being heavily used at peak periods.

. . . features a service which brings the Rhondda commuters to the Capital City of Wales

Corn Stores Hill and Taff Street, Pontypridd . . . . Porth . . . . Wattstown Colliery . . . . and so to the terminus—Ferndale

1963 JUNE Staff BULLETIN — The Staff Magazine of the Western Welsh Omnibus Company Limited

An Atlantean passes Barry Island funfair with its Big Dipper.

A feature of the *Bulletins* was a series of pictures covering individual routes, which give a good idea of the company's operating territory. This one shows the 330.

POSITION OF ROL…

Depot		No.	Vehicles
BARRY	◆	43	13 14 150 239 247 258 270 273 / 604 605 606 702 703 704 705 722 / 775 776 777
BRECON	●	15	23 24 121 136 143 169 177 19…
BRIDGEND	▲	94	1 5 7 18 19 20 50 51 / 117 118 120 145 146 147 148 15… / 241 248 249 251 254 265 271 27… / 401 402 469 538 549 550 564 56… / 590 591 592 717 718 719 739 7…
PORTTALBOT		9	161 164 166 170 183 297 403 5…
CARDIFF	▲	46	133 204 285 286 330 331 332 3… / 581 582 583 584 594 595 596 5… / 746 750 753 755 778 779
CROSSKEYS	■	72	6 26 27 28 29 30 53 / 153 174 175 176 180 193 194 / 256 260 264 266 267 268 269 / 701 727 728 729 737 747 748
CARM AREA	■	~~87~~ (89)	12 15 16 17 43 45 46 / ~~75~~ Dick 76 78 79 80 81 82 / 123 124 127 131 137 144 156 / 303 306 308 314 318 319 320 ~~410~~ / 487 488 738 764 765 766 767 105 ~~97~~
NEATH	◆	37	62 106 173 181 182 190 192 201 225 227 252 279 280 281 282 283 284 290 291 309 / 310 311 457 458 568 607 713 714 731 732 740 741 769 770 C [illegible] C [illegible] C [illegible]
ABERDARE		19	8 11 21 22 186 188 221 228 353 358 477 489 491 492 493 494 495 710 711
AMMANFORD		14	119 128 129 152 155 179 185 226 235 289 313 334 712 715
PONTYPOOL	●	45	25 42 48 49 125 126 130 132 135 138 139 140 142 151 157 158 187 195 196 197 / 208 210 222 230 231 242 243 244 259 261 262 263 322 323 324 325 327 328 720 721 / 730 743 C 1149 C 1160 C 1176
DELICENCED FOR BODY CONVERSION		10 ~~11~~ ~~9~~ ~~10~~	2 3 4 9 ~~10~~ 44 56 57 77 ~~97~~ ~~97~~ ~~105~~
" RETENTION.		2	108 216
" DISPOSAL		~~23~~	~~351~~ ~~362~~ ~~359~~ ~~360~~ ~~361~~ ~~362~~ ~~363~~ ~~364~~ ~~365~~ ~~377~~ ~~379~~ ~~380~~ ~~381~~ ~~394~~ ~~454~~ ~~455~~ ~~456~~ ~~459~~ ~~462~~ ~~465~~ / ~~466~~ ~~468~~ ~~481~~
		~~493~~ 516	— Jan 1st 1946

Allocation of Rolling Stock

April 1, 1963

Depot		Allocation Code	Coaches	Semi-coaches	Saloons	Double-decked	Total
			No. of Vehicles				
Brecon		White Diamond	—	1	13	—	
Abergavenny	o/s	,, ,,	—	—	4	—	19
Hay-on-Wye	o/s	,, ,,	—	—	1	—	
Pontypool		White Diamond	2	4	72	—	
Varteg Hill	o/s	,, ,,	—	—	10	—	88
Cross Keys		Yellow Diamond	7	2	31	27	67
Cardiff		Orange Diamond	22	11	8	30	71
Barry		Black Diamond	4	2	24	29	59
Bridgend		Blue Diamond	2	3	69	12	
Port Talbot		,, ,,	—	—	14	—	
Porthcawl	o/s	,, ,,	—	—	—	1	106
Kenfig Hill	o/s	,, ,,	—	—	2	2	
Glyncorrwg	o/s	,, ,,	—	—	—	1	
Neath		Red Diamond	10	5	8	6	
Aberdare		,, ,,	—	2	16	4	
Ammanford		,, ,,	—	—	10	4	
Llanelly	o/s	,, ,,	—	—	1	—	70
Lampeter	o/s	,, ,,	—	—	2	—	
Aberystwyth	o/s	,, ,,	—	—	1	—	
Porthcawl	o/s	,, ,,	—	—	1	—	
Haverfordwest		Green Diamond	3	5	15	19	
Milford Haven		,, ,,	—	—	5	3	
St. David's		,, ,,	—	—	9	3	
Fishguard		,, ,,	—	—	4	—	
Carmarthen		,, ,,	3	1	14	1	
Newcastle Emlyn		,, ,,	—	—	6	1	
New Quay		,, ,,	—	—	7	—	
Pontyberem		,, ,,	—	—	4	—	115
Neyland		,, ,,	—	—	1	1	
Llangwm	o/s	,, ,,	—	—	1	—	
Saundersfoot	o/s	,, ,,	—	—	1	—	
Narberth	o/s	,, ,,	—	—	1	—	
Freystrop	o/s	,, ,,	—	—	1		
Llandyssul	o/s	,, ,,	—		1	—	
Laugharne	o/s	,, ,,	—	—	4	1	
Ely Works		,, ,,	11	14	40	18	83
Total Fleet			64	50	401	163	678

Western Welsh Vehicle Allocation, April 1963.

8. All Change on the Buses

It is difficult to know where to start. Following World War 2 a shift in the relationship between employees and employers was accompanied by higher expectations, perhaps most vividly evidenced by the shock defeat of Winston Churchill in the 1945 General Election. Additional benefits were sought — and gained — in the prevailing political climate, usually by negotiation within joint bodies. All these added to costs. In October 1951 R. T. E. estimated that with a wage increase these had added £124,000 per annum to the company's costs. He urged all staff to adhere to the slogan 'one more passenger per mile'. Whereas these costs were, to an extent, within the industry's control, fuel tax was not. As restrictions on petrol supply eased, people naturally wanted to reacquaint themselves with motoring, either as they had done prewar or as they had learned during the war. Governments of all hues were quick to see an opportunity here and started to rack up fuel tax at an alarming rate. In April 1950 it was doubled, and 12 months later a further increase cost Western Welsh £118,000 per annum. This resulted in the first-ever fares increase, which did not go down too well. 'We have all experienced increases in the prices of everything we use — clothing, coal, electricity, gas, rates, food (including beer) and even railway travel — without all this fuss and bother. Until the present time, bus fares have been the only everyday commodity available at prewar prices. It is not politics, tell your passengers,' thundered R. T. E. in March 1951. And it wasn't going to be the last. In March 1952 7½d extra on a gallon on the company's two million gallons a year added another £70,000 per annum. 'Wallop!' cried R. T. E. 'Try and conserve this liquid gold.' He had noted in June 1950 that it was not only the tax impact on the company; as more passengers used cars rather than buses this would lead to reduced revenue and increased congestion. How different it might have been if governments had seen the importance of buses and eased or even removed the tax. The inexorable decline had begun.

And then there was bus design. Just before and during World War 2 the BMMO ('Midland Red') company in Birmingham, which built its own buses, had devised a design of saloon which had the engine under the floor and, extended to the new maximum length of 30ft, could hold 44 passengers with a door right at the front, supervised by the driver. It was revolutionary, and, given the huge benefits it offered in a climate of massive cost increases, other operators put strong pressure on manufacturers to produce something similar for the open market. By 1951 this was a reality, and front-engined single-deckers became obsolete overnight. As did Western Welsh's brand-spanking-new fleet. And there still remained much catching-up to do to counter the shortage of new buses over the war years. If all this were not enough, R. T. E.'s 'Wallop' editorial would turn out to be his last. A well-regarded and popular General Manager at Western Welsh and respected throughout the industry, he died on 3 April 1952, after a short illness, in Llandough Hospital near Cardiff. Challenging times lay ahead.

◂◂ WW used a unique system of diamonds to show the allocation of the vehicle. Originally these had different shapes within them, but this was later simplified to different colours.
Chris Taylor; Viv Corbin

"48 *m.p.h. is bad enough, but when he asks for your name and address, and you says, 'Regd. T. Ebrey, c/o Western Welsh Offices, Ely'—well, that's asking for trouble!*"

▲ Cartoon from the *Bulletin* of October 1951.

◂ A cartoon from the *Bulletin* of August 1965, predating Doctor Who's move to Cardiff.

9. There's Something about a Tiger Cub

'We are in the process of taking delivery of a new type of single-deck bus to the 30ft x 8ft dimensions,' announced the Chief Engineer in May 1951. He went on to explain that the buses were of integral (or 'chassisless') all-metal construction, whereby the major units were attached to the body and could not be separated from it as on earlier buses. 'The panels play an important part in the strength of the structure, as can be seen by the size of the rivets used in securing them to the main pillars,' he further explained. The engine, mounted underfloor, gave it 'the same power as a PD2/3 double-deck'; it had twin heaters, folding doors controlled by the driver and 44 forward-facing seats with a wider gangway to 'facilitate movement of conductor and passengers'. This official study of 404, the first of 10, was recorded at Llandaff Cathedral in Cardiff and is notable in that the bus has its manufacturer's badge on the front. WW would not have allowed it to enter service like this; the 'LEYLAND' badges on the company's Titans, for example, were replaced by cast-iron plates proclaiming the company name. *David Kershaw collection*

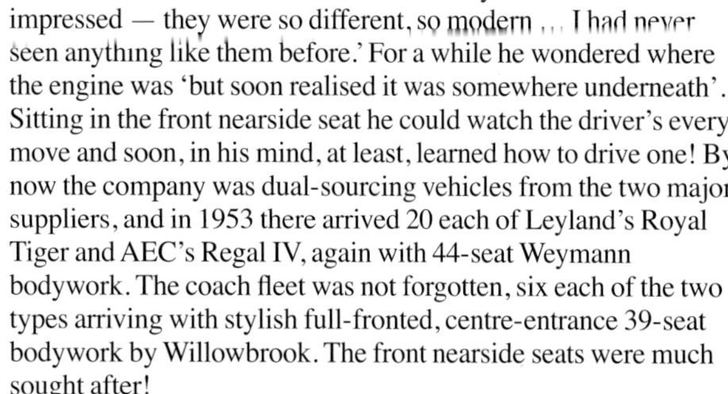

Manufacturers approached the new underfloor-engined era in different ways. Initially, integral buses, with running units suspended from a body structure, making them chassisless, were thought to be the way forward. Western Welsh was quick off the mark, taking 10 of Leyland's offering, the Olympic, in mid-1951. However, operators were wary, generally preferring the choice of body on separate chassis, and at the same time Western Welsh took 25 of Leyland's version of that, the Royal Tiger, albeit with the same 44-seat Weymann bodywork. Alan Roberts grew up near Neath and used to holiday in St Dogmaels, travelling there by bus. It was on one of these epic journeys that he first encountered these buses. 'I was very impressed — they were so different, so modern ... I had never seen anything like them before.' For a while he wondered where the engine was 'but soon realised it was somewhere underneath'. Sitting in the front nearside seat he could watch the driver's every move and soon, in his mind, at least, learned how to drive one! By now the company was dual-sourcing vehicles from the two major suppliers, and in 1953 there arrived 20 each of Leyland's Royal Tiger and AEC's Regal IV, again with 44-seat Weymann bodywork. The coach fleet was not forgotten, six each of the two types arriving with stylish full-fronted, centre-entrance 39-seat bodywork by Willowbrook. The front nearside seats were much sought after!

The new arrivals gave much-needed extra capacity but had one snag: they were incredibly thirsty, at a time when fuel was becoming an increasingly expensive commodity. Added to which, the Royal Tiger had a reluctance to stop. Manufacturers were soon under pressure to look at ways of shedding weight. Leyland's answer was the Tiger Cub, almost two tons lighter, powered by the economical O.350 engine whilst still carrying the sleek, modern 44-seat Weymann body. Alan Roberts remembers these as being more rounded, having softer corners 'as though all the rough edges had been removed'. Detailed tests using 10 of these buses in tough operating conditions showed a consumption of 14.12 miles per gallon, a saving of 2.42mpg over other types of underfloor-engined buses, which translated into a saving of £150 per month. Operators today would give their eye teeth for fuel-usage figures as good as these! The 10 were part of an order for 50 that began to arrive in late 1953. Western Welsh clearly felt it needed look no further, promptly ordering 80 more, and delivery of all 130 was complete by the end of 1954, a creditable performance. It was the start of something special that led to an eventual fleet of 349 Tiger Cubs, the largest in the UK and probably anywhere. Indeed, the early examples would be replaced by later buses of the same type — a rare occurrence! However, the company did not entirely turn its back on integrals, for in 1954 a solitary Olympian, the second prototype of this new Leyland model, again with 44-seat Weymann bodywork and present at that year's Commercial Motor Show, joined the teeming hordes of Tiger Cubs.

The Tiger Cubs appear to have come in the nick of time. By 1952/3 profits had halved to £103,599; in 1953/4, with the fleet standing at a total of 627 buses, they soared back up to £211,330.

▲ One of the 20 AEC Regal IVs with Weymann bodies that came along in 1953, 544 in Cardiff is in the modified single-deck livery without the upper cream band as seen on 545 below. The shot also shows the large WW names on the bus station buildings, then home to Head Office. *Chris Taylor collection*

▲ Revolutionary new coaches came in 1953 on underfloor-engined coach chassis with 39-seat centre-entrance bodywork by Willowbrook. Six each of Leyland's and AEC's offerings were bought, 521, one of the former, being seen at Carmarthen in July 1963. *Viv Corbin collection*

▲ An interesting line-up of buses at British Resin Products' Barry factory in 1955 shows three types of WW bus of the time. No 545 was one of the 44-seat Regal IVs, 653 a 53-seat lowbridge Regent and 774 a 56-seat highbridge Leyland Titan TD7 originally intended for Southdown. It neatly illustrates a thoughtful article penned by Owain G. Davies in the October 1952 *Bulletin* wherein he considered the impact of the new 44-seaters. Whilst adding a number of caveats, he did make the interesting observation that in a fleet of 300, fifty 53-seat and fifty 56-seat double-deckers, along with a hundred each of 32- and 35-seater single-deckers, would give a total seating capacity of 12,150, while three hundred 44-seaters would provide 13,200 seats. Those 44-seaters certainly caused a stir. *Viv Corbin collection*

▲ A picture that sums up Western Welsh. Some 180 of these Weymann-bodied Tiger Cubs formed the mainstay of the fleet for many years and could be found throughout the patch. Seen in Pontypool, 1052, representing the first 130 examples, stands next to 1151, one of the next 50, with more rounded and even sleeker bodywork. *Chris Taylor collection*

10. The 'Fifties. Yes, well . . .

A 1948 Brush-bodied AEC Regent III heads for the bus station in Cardiff. These buses had substantial rear bumpers but no rear destination screen. A motor bus and trolleybus of Cardiff Corporation are further down St Mary Street; if WW's bid in 1951 had been successful, they would have been owned by different firms. There's a lovely Ford Anglia 100E stopped at the zebra crossing in this typical mid-'50s scene.
Chris Taylor collection

Western Welsh entered the 1950s with much the same approach to life but in circumstances that were much changed. A bold move in January 1951 was a £350,000 offer for Cardiff Corporation's motor-bus fleet. Note just the motor buses; Cardiff had just invested heavily in a modern fleet of trolleybuses and, had the deal come off, it would have been most interesting to see how the two systems would have interacted. It didn't.

In July 1951, in a ceremony described by R. T. E. as 'a unique and proud occasion' for the company, the Mayor of Barry presented two locally based members of staff with certificates awarded by the 'Order of the Knights of the Road' to recognise acts of courtesy. A third followed in August 1952.

The registered office moved in March 1952 to Stratton House in London and then, in October, to the company's offices at 253 Cowbridge Road West in Ely (the first time it had been in the 'patch'), although Directors' meetings were still held at Stratton House. Capital was increased for the first time, rising from £500,000 to £1,268,750 in 1953 and again to £1,624,000 in 1954. In June T. G. Davies returned from Rhondda as General Manager, and in December Leslie Gray became Assistant Chief Engineer. The Gray dynasty had briefly increased in 1946 when his brother, Ivor, returned from war service as an area manager, but he had soon accepted the post of General Manager of Hebble Motor Services in Halifax. He was to return! In March 1955 Albert Gray finally severed his direct contact with the company, resigning his consultancy post at the age of 75! Another long connection ended a year previously with the retirement of Albert E. Smith, the Parcels Manager.

An interesting development in June 1952 was the start of a service to Rhoose Airport (now Cardiff International) to connect with Aer Lingus flights to Dublin which prompted a *Bulletin* article about transport co-ordination!

Some BET activities at this time were to have a great influence on Western Welsh. In November 1950 the group had bought James of Ammanford, in April 1951 Neath & Cardiff Luxury Coaches, and in April 1953 Thomas Bros of Port Talbot. Western Welsh became responsible for heavy overhauls and body transfers, as well as checking new buses (and disposing of

A fabulous picture from the *Bulletin*, taken in the mid-1960s from Cardiff Corporation's offices overlooking the bus station. WW buses are in the centre with Rhondda's to the left and Red & White's to the right. More WWs can be seen alongside the offices, while Neath & Cardiff coaches are at the far end. Glory days indeed! *David Kershaw collection*

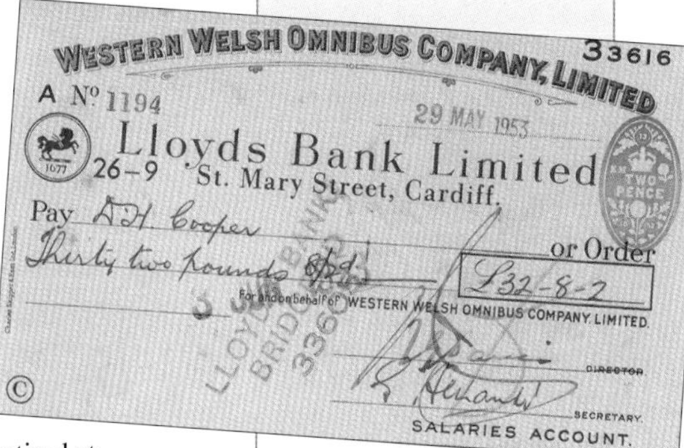

WESTERN WELSH OMNIBUS COMPANY, LIMITED 33616

A Nº 1194 29 MAY 1953

Lloyds Bank Limited

26–9 St. Mary Street, Cardiff.

TWO PENCE

Pay D.H. Cooper or Order

Thirty two pounds 8/2d £32-8-2

For and on behalf of WESTERN WELSH OMNIBUS COMPANY LIMITED.

DIRECTOR

SECRETARY.

SALARIES ACCOUNT.

Cheque, 1953. *Chris Taylor collection*

old ones) for James. Indeed, new vehicles for the James fleet were often to be seen at Cowbridge Road, which makes that company's absorption by South Wales (in 1962) somewhat surprising, particularly as its fleet was more akin to that of Western Welsh. The latter also garaged six N&C coaches in Cardiff. Thomas Bros became very efficient and took over some Western Welsh routes in Port Talbot.

Work continued on the buildings front: in 1954 extensions to the tune of £8,500 were made to Ely Works, and a new garage, at a cost of £12,230 (including the freehold of the land), was opened in St David's. The building in St David's could house 12 buses, and the first supervisor was Mr E. E. Hurley, who had charge of 42 staff, 10 saloons, four double-deckers and a coach. In December of the same year buses moved into the fine new bus station in Cardiff, where Head Office staff were to join them in 1957. Western Welsh was responsible for 102,149 of the 395,719 bus departures made annually. Another new bus station, this time in Newport, opened in 1959. Extensions were made to Barry, Bridgend and Crosskeys depots, plans were made for a depot in the proposed new town of Cwmbran, and a new depot in Neath came on stream in 1957. The last was built in 15 months for the sum of £51,771 and replaced former GWR premises at Riverside, Cadoxton, that had served the company since 1931. The new building housed 30 buses, and there was room for a further 50 on adjoining land. It served as the control for Ammanford and Aberdare depots, also under the supervision of Area Manager W. J. Jones, with a combined staff of 326 and a fleet of 82. Shortly before it opened the company's architect, Mr E. Webster, who had brought a very clear company style to WW's buildings, retired at the age of 78, after a career lasting 67 years. If that were not enough, a six-vehicle depot in Fishguard, costing £20,000, opened in August 1959.

Takeovers continued, and two themes seemed to run through them. An unsuccessful attempt was made to buy Thomas Bros of Barry, which, following a route swap with Red & White, remained Western Welsh's only competitor on routes to Barry.

Official Opening

BY THE

CHAIRMAN OF THE LICENSING AUTHORITY
OF THE SOUTH WALES TRAFFIC AREA
(C. R. HODGSON, Esq., O.B.E.)

OF THE

NEW GARAGE AT ST. DAVID'S,
PEMBS.

On THURSDAY, 16th DECEMBER, 1954

WESTERN WELSH

NEW GARAGE

NEATH

JULY - 1957

Brochures for the opening of St David's and Neath depots. As the former was near Christmas, the celebratory meal was turkey with all the trimmings! *Viv Corbin collection*

▲ On 19 April 1954 Leyland TS8 No 315 passes Eastbrook railway station on the 'low road' to Barry via Dinas Powys, shared with Thomas Motors and Reliance of Barry. The reliance part became the subject of a rare route swap with Red & White but Thomas refused to sell. Fitted with a 32 seat Brush body, this bus spent its entire career from 1939 until 1956 based at Barry. *Alan Jarvis*

◄ As no premises were involved in the Ebsworth purchase, buses had to be parked out in the open. A few were kept at Laugharne for use on the Pendine service. Seen in the yard there is 1306, a 1963 Tiger Cub PSUC1/11 with Marshall bodywork built at a time when the BET Federation design had reached a depth of blandness. Bridgemaster 686 is at the yard in July 1966. *Chris Taylor collection; Roger Davies* ►

Otherwise, apart from a route between Kenfig and Porthcawl in 1953, acquisitions tended to be in the west. Ebsworth Bros of Laugharne was associated with the Hodge Group. This had been set up by South Wales entrepreneur Julian Hodge, a former railway man, as was T. G. Davies. Mr Hodge rang Mr Davies and a deal was struck. With 11 buses, mainly Leylands, it fitted in quite well, being bought in December 1954 for £27,500. As no premises were included, buses were parked in a small yard in the town, plans for a depot coming to naught. But probably the most significant purchase was that of Green's Motors of Haverfordwest, which wanted to sell as a result of death duties. This brought premises and 44 buses for £55,000. Further property was bought in the town for £14,000, and Western Welsh overnight became a major player in the area. Although the fleet looked good, much of it wasn't, and public complaints started to roll in. Apparently the buses were acceptable as Green's but not as Western Welsh! Many had to be replaced by company stock, and the management was chided over its actions. Some of the buses were fine, however, and a number of AECs and Leylands went on to enjoy long lives with their new owners, often remaining local and thus giving the place a distinctive air. In 1959 the bus services of Prendergast Motors in Haverfordwest and T. J. Harries & Sons in Milford Haven were added for a total of £20,000.

Clearly, Western Welsh felt that this was an area set to expand economically as a result of the rapidly growing oil industry at Milford Haven, one of only two British ports deep enough to take the new generation of supertankers. But it must be said that its assessment looks a bit odd when viewed in the light of General Manager T. G. Davies' comments in the July 1956 *Bulletin*. 'The serious financial losses being sustained by omnibus companies operating rural services is a topic that is given a regular airing in the Traffic Courts these days.' Appearances in said courts were becoming more commonplace as fares increases became more frequent; that of 1953, only the company's second and designed to counter costs that had risen 150% since before the war, brought a lot of complaints and an objection to the Minister of Transport from local authorities.

Mr Davies went on: 'This company operates a large number of rural services. Most of them do not pay and never will, and their continued survival is due to the fact they are subsidised by industrial services that continue to pay.' These were significant words, and the GM also flagged up the likelihood of one-man buses, 64 rural services being converted to that form of operation in 1959. The profitable services used to prop up the West Wales loss-makers were a long way away from most of them.

▲ Among the ex-Green's buses was 383, a 1949 Guy Arab III with low-height Barnard bodywork. Here it is at Ely, just repainted; subsequently it would have its Meadows engine replaced by a Gardner 6LW, lasting thus until 1959. *G. H. Truran / Richard Saunders collection*

◄ No 989, an all-Leyland PD1 dating from 1947, was one of the vehicles acquired in 1956 with Green's of Haverfordwest and was very soon painted into WW livery. Seen here at the depot with a Guy still in Green's livery, it lasted until December 1959. *Chris Taylor collection*

No 993, an all-Leyland PD2/12, the only one of this type in the WW fleet, came with Green's, having been bought by that company in June 1954. It retained Green's livery until September 1957 but is seen here in WW all-over red, working a Haverfordwest town service. It lasted until 1969. *[Chris Taylor collection* ▸

▲ No 682, a 1949 AEC Regent III with Cardiff-built Bruce bodywork, was one of two that came from Green's. It was refurbished in 1957, thereafter spending a few years at Cardiff, where it is seen here. In 1960 it returned to Haverfordwest until withdrawal in 1962. *Chris Taylor collection*

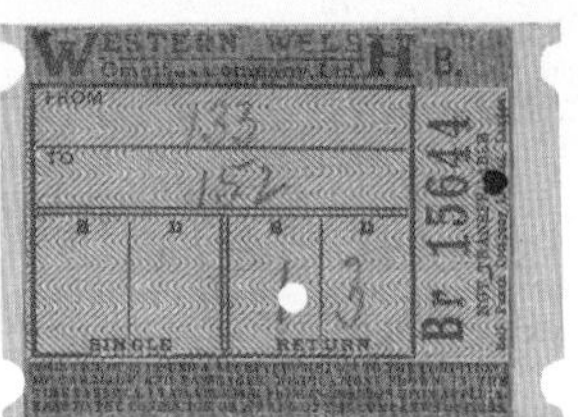

Bellgraphic ticket. *Viv Corbin collection*

WW timetable with political slogan, 1955. *Viv Corbin collection*

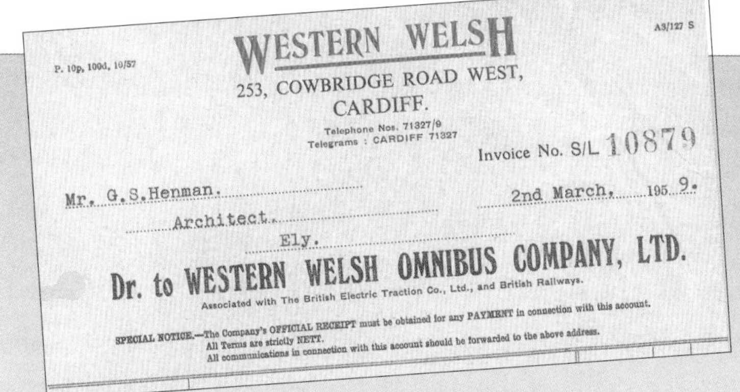

P. 10p, 100d, 10/57

A3/127 S

WESTERN WELSH
253, COWBRIDGE ROAD WEST,
CARDIFF.

Telephone Nos. 71327/9
Telegrams : CARDIFF 71327

Invoice No. S/L 10879

Mr. G.S.Henman. 2nd March, 195 9.
Architect.
Ely.

Dr. to WESTERN WELSH OMNIBUS COMPANY, LTD.

Associated with The British Electric Traction Co., Ltd., and British Railways.

SPECIAL NOTICE.—The Company's OFFICIAL RECEIPT must be obtained for any PAYMENT in connection with this account.
All Terms are strictly NETT.
All communications in connection with this account should be forwarded to the above address.

An order form from 1959.

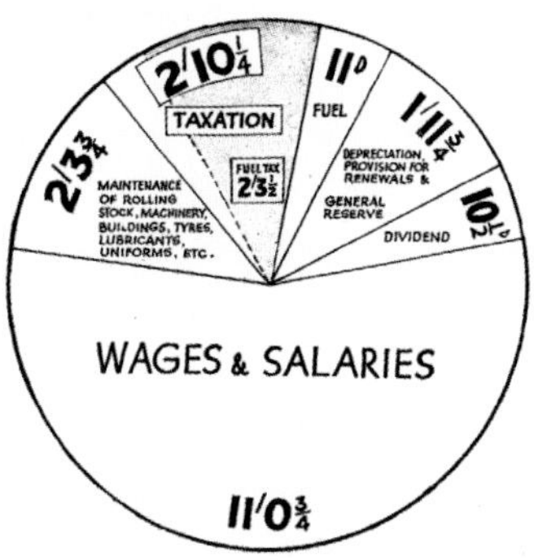

The revenue split, 1955.

Kz 7692

WESTERN WELSH OMNIBUS CO. LTD.
WEEKLY TICKET VALID FOR
6
DAYS TRAVEL
DURING WEEK OF ISSUE ONLY.

Not Valid Unless Price Printed

A weekly ticket. *Viv Corbin collection*

Taken over with Green's, 595, one of two Strachans-bodied Regal IIIs new in March 1950, spent some time at Barry before ending its days back in Haverfordwest. It was sold in September 1960. *Kenneth Evans collection*

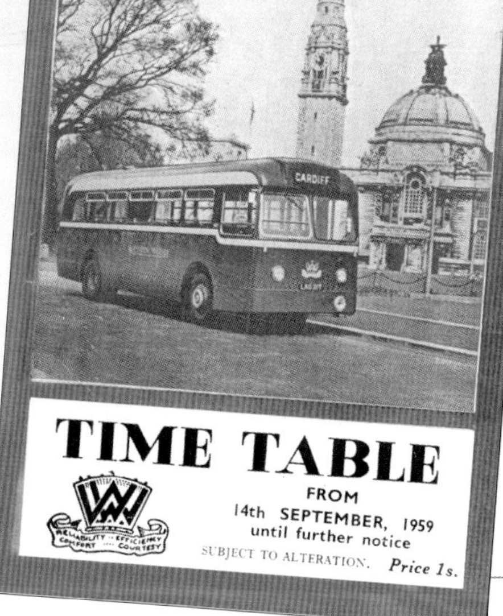

WW timetable, 1959. What better mission statement than 'Reliability, Efficiency, Comfort, Courtesy'? *Viv Corbin collection*

O. CO. LTD. WESTERN WELSH O.

SEE OVER. FOR CONDITIONS SE

A Setright ticket, as used from 1956. Setright machines were introduced in October 1956 at Brecon and Carmarthen and soon spread to other depots. *Viv Corbin collection*

▲ This excellent photograph shows the short-lived depot at Albert Road, Penarth, taken over in June 1954 with the business of Streamways Ltd. After a few seasons' use it was sold in March 1962. The unique coach shown here is the 1952 Regal IV chassis acquired with Cridlands, which WW fitted with a 34-seat Willowbrook body in 1955. This was an appropriate location as its number, 539, was that allocated to the phantom fourth vehicle that should have come from Streamways! *Viv Corbin collection*

◄ Photographed on the ramp at Cowbridge Road, with the County cinema across the road, 538 was a Commer Avenger with Plaxton bodywork, bought with Streamways of Penarth in 1954. Although painted up in livery as here, it was used by WW for only two months, ultimately being sold — for £350 — in 1956. Indicative of a rather sorry tale. *Chris Taylor collection*

A 17-vehicle private hire on 24 August 1955 was organised to transport the Mormon Tabernacle Choir the short distance from Cardiff General station to Sophia Gardens, where they gave a concert, and thence to the Civic Centre. The coaches used included were among those acquired the previous year with the business of Cridlands of Cardiff. They included EBO 800, one of the four Maudslays taken over, and, third in line, GKG 600, a petrol-engined Bedford SB. Numbered 569, it was licensed by WW only for the months of July and August 1955. Note the period dual-windtone horns. On the left of the picture is the old GWR parcels depot. And just look at that superb Wolseley 6/80 police car. *Viv Corbin collection* ►

The other theme was coaches. Western Welsh felt that the leisure market could make up for the decline in the bus side of the business; indeed, Fred Pengelly wanted the company to be the prime coach operator in South East Wales. £20,000 was paid in April 1954 for Streamways coaches of Penarth, apparently bringing four vehicles, a depot and excursion and tour licences. This was not without its problems on the financial side, and the company's management was censured for allowing Streamways to default on debts, a situation compounded by the fact that there were, in fact, only three vehicles. Cliff Wiltshire, who worked in the Cost Office at Ely, recalled that on visiting the Streamways site he found nothing — not even a spanner! It was wound up with no assets. Two months later Cridlands of Cardiff was bought again with E&T licences and a fleet of 10 coaches, this time costing £15,000. This deal was not without its problems either, evidenced by the fact that an 11th vehicle was a chassis only; Western Welsh had a coach body fitted the following year. These operators brought in some familiar types of AEC and Leyland but also included Bedfords, Maudslays and, harking back to the company's origins, a Commer. Interestingly they brought back into the fleet four petrol-engined coaches, including a very thirsty 7.4-litre Maudslay Marathon 2. Then, in April 1956, E. R. Forse of Cardiff was bought for £75,000, bringing in 21 coaches made up of AECs, Daimlers, Dennises, Crossleys, a single Foden and a rather fine new depot in Blackweir. To be perfectly honest, Western Welsh didn't seem to quite know what to do with it.

On 1 July 1959, alongside the company's offices in Market Street, Bridgend, coach 567 waits to depart on an afternoon trip to the Brecon Beacons. Perhaps the gent on the left is looking for the 7s 6d (37p) fare. The coach is a Maudslay Marathon III with 37-seat Plaxton Envoy bodywork, dating from 1951. It came with the Cridlands business and lasted with WW until 1961. *Viv Corbin collection*

▲ With the takeover in April 1956 of E. R. Forse of Cardiff came this unusual vehicle — a 30ft-long Dennis Lancet J10 with 37-seat coach body by Welsh coachbuilder D. J. Davies, new in March 1951. Numbered 593 by WW, it ran from Blackweir garage for two seasons before being sold late in 1957 to Thorpe's Coaches of London. *Chris Taylor / Peter Smith collection*

◄ Forse's livery was an immaculate grey, blue and cream. Pictured outside its operator's new garage in Blackweir is FBO 690, an AEC Regal III of 1950 with a Harrington body complete with dorsal fin. It became WW 581 in 1956, and for some reason the fin was removed. It gained cream and red at first, then DP livery, and was based at Bridgend. It was withdrawn in 1961. *Chris Taylor collection*

A rare colour shot of ex-Forse HBO 700 in all-over cream as WW 588. A Daimler Freeline with Plaxton body, this magnificent coach was a bit of a heavyweight (at over 8 tons!) and unfortunately proved unreliable. It lasted until 1962. *Chris Taylor collection*

E. R. Forse leaflet. Note, all total abstainers. *Peter Smith collection*

Open Day and Night. Phone 27506 (2 lines)

E. R. FORSE

Kingsway Garage, Cardiff

MOTOR COACH HIRE SERVICE

My Grey and Blue Super Coaches are available for

OUTINGS . . . DANCES . . TOURS.

ANY NUMBER CATERED FOR :: EXPERT DRIVERS :: TOTAL ABSTAINERS

Passing the Head Office at 253 Cowbridge Road West, Ely, ex-Forse EKG 650 (now WW 579) has the famous 'dorsal fin' 33-seat Harrington body. This was removed in 1959, when 579 was relegated to dual-purpose duties for its final two years with the company. *Kenneth Evans collection*

Nevertheless, the company was now a major provider of excursions, and in the early 1970s it would fall to a young Roger Davies to call in shunters, fitters, driving instructors and Head Office staff to cover the programme on busy days. Excursions could have some interesting consequences. Alan Roberts recalls Horace from his local depot of Neath, who had a reputation for getting lost, doing just that on a trip and ending up in a side road stuck behind some sheep. A passenger guided him back to the main road, but at their destination they had time only for a quick ice cream before heading for home. Oh, the trip? It was a mystery tour!

Western Welsh also started to build up a much-admired programme of extended tours, with a coach fleet to match. These tours were meticulously planned, and the Gray family travelled on them, with Leslie, a keen photographer, filming the sights. These films were shown during winter months to prospective clients. Thankfully, much of this early cine film has been preserved by the Grays and is safely stored in the National Library of Wales in Aberystwyth. Western Welsh coach tours stuck to the mainland, leaving foreign travel to nearby South Wales. However, a fascinating tour was mounted to Northern Ireland, where an Ulster Transport Authority coach was used. Roger Davies remembers a smart red-and-ivory coach pulling up outside the house — yes, really — to take his grandparents to the Kyles of Bute or some such exotica, while Stephen Barber recalls that in his days at NBC in the 1970s Western Welsh tours were always held in the highest regard. But pride of place goes to a Lakes and Scotland tour in October 1963. On board was Bridgend driver E. C. White, recuperating after a period in hospital, who sat, by sheer chance, next to a Miss Gillian Barrow. Six months later they wed. And their honeymoon? The Lakes and Scotland — with the same driver!

Notwithstanding these exploits, whatever the company did, profits in the late 1950s languished at between £100,000 and £150,000, and it was a very seasonal, heavily cross-subsidised outfit that entered the 1960s. It was going to be a bumpy ride.

◄ Tours brochure, 1950.
Viv Corbin collection

Tours brochure, 1954. ►
Viv Corbin collection

▲ Six Reliances with Harrington bodywork arrived in 1964. This stylised picture of 144 in Sedlescombe, Sussex, featured in that year's tour brochure. *Viv Corbin collection*

WESTERN WELSH

Luxury Coach Tours

1964

Cover of the 1964 tours brochure, featuring a Reliance/Weymann beside Loch Lomond. *Viv Corbin collection*

Itinerary for the Northern Ireland tour, introduced in 1961. *Viv Corbin collection* ▸

ENGLISH LAKES AND NORTHERN IRELAND

THE character of Northern Ireland is one of welcome, and this is true not only of the people but also of the countryside. The smiling fields and the rolling hills are never far distant and they have a soft and green quality. In this new tour we link a visit to this delightful country with a short stay in the English Lake district.

After spending a night at Grange-over-Sands, the Morecambe Bay resort, we make for Scotland and Ayr on the south-west coast, which has many associations with the poet Robert Burns.

At Stranraer we board the steamer which takes us across the water to Larne Harbour, from where we journey to the seaside resort of Portrush. We visit the Giant's Causeway, Ulster's show-piece and a sight which once seen is never likely to be forgotten. The world-famous cliffs of black basalt, formed into columns, usually six-sided in section, form an amazing natural phenomenon.

Next we see something of the famous Glens of Antrim, nine glacier-worn valleys, smooth as the inside of a boat, which carry gurgling trout streams towards the sea. Before leaving Northern Ireland we spend some time at Belfast, on the mouth of the River Lagan. The largest city in Northern Ireland and the seat of government, Belfast has many attractions for the visitor.

Returning to Stranraer we wend our way back to the border and make for the beautiful Lake District where we pause awhile before continuing by way of Lancaster to Preston, Whitchurch, Shrewsbury, Leominster and more familiar countryside.

DEPARTURES FROM :

PORT TALBOT (Bethany Square)	7.50 a.m.
BRIDGEND ('Bus Station)	8.20 a.m.
CARDIFF (Central 'Bus Station)	9.30 a.m.
NEWPORT ('Bus Station)	10.05 a.m.

EACH SUNDAY—

JUNE 4th to SEPTEMBER 3rd (Inclusive)

Fare £28 10s. 0d. (Inclusive of First-Class Steamer Fare)

30

Sunday Leave CARDIFF, Newport, MONMOUTH (Coffee), Hereford, Leominster, LUDLOW (Lunch, Feathers Hotel), Church Stretton, Shrewsbury, STOCKTON HEATH (Tea, Victoria Hotel), Warrington, Preston, Lancaster, GRANGE-OVER-SANDS (Dinner, Night, Grand Hotel).

Monday Leave Hotel 9.00 a.m., via Newby Bridge, Windermere, PATTERDALE (Coffee), Penrith, CARLISLE (Lunch, Crown and Mitre Hotel), Dumfries, CASTLE DOUGLAS (Tea, Ken Bridge Hotel), New Galloway, Dalmellington, AYR (Dinner, Night, Station Hotel).

Tuesday Morning free for individual action. Lunch at Hotel. Depart 1.45 p.m., via Turnberry, Girvan, Ballantrae, STRANRAER (Tea and Dinner, George Hotel). Party will board Steamer after Dinner. First Class Cabins have been reserved on Steamer which will sail at 7.00 a.m., on Wednesday morning.

Wednesday Steamer crossing from STRANRAER to LARNE HARBOUR (arrive 9.30 a.m.), then by coach via BALLYMENA (Coffee), Kilrea, Bann Valley, Coleraine, Portstewart, PORTRUSH (Lunch, Northern Counties Hotel), Bushmills, GIANT'S CAUSEWAY (Tea, Causeway Hotel), Ballycastle, Cushendale, Ballymon Glen, Parkmore, GLENARIFF GLEN, Waterfoot, Carnlough, Glenarm, LARNE (Dinner, Night, Laharna Hotel).

Thursday Leave Hotel 9.15 a.m., via Ballynure, Glengormley, Belfast, Carryduff, Ballynahinch, NEWCASTLE (Lunch, Slieve Donard Hotel), Bryansford, Spelga Pass, Kilkeel, ROSTREVOR (Tea, Great Northern Hotel), Warrenpoint, Newry, Banbridge, Dromore, Hillsborough, Lisburn, BELFAST (Dinner, Night, Belgravia Hotel).

Friday Leave Hotel 7.15 a.m., via Carrickfergus, Whitehead, LARNE HARBOUR (Steamer departs 8.30 a.m.), STRANRAER (Lunch, George Hotel), Newton Stewart, Castle Douglas, DUMFRIES (Tea, King's Arms Hotel), Carlisle, Penrith, Kendal, WINDERMERE (Dinner, Night, Hydro Hotel).

Saturday Leave Hotel 9.00 a.m., via LANCASTER (Coffee), Preston, Warrington, STOCKTON HEATH (Lunch, Victoria Hotel), Whitchurch, Shrewsbury, Ludlow, LEOMINSTER (Tea, Talbot Hotel), Hereford, Monmouth, Newport, CARDIFF (arrive 8.30 p.m. approx.).

BRIG O'DOON AND BURNS MONUMENT

Photo by The Scottish Tourist Board

31

Excursions from Cowbridge, 1966.
Viv Corbin collection

A Reliance/Plaxton parked at its overnight stop in 1970.
Christine Davies collection

No 148, one of the 1964 Reliance/Harrington coaches and its clients at Heathrow Airport in 1967.
Christine Davies collection

The run from Bridgend to Southerndown, introduced in 1922, was and remains a spectacular journey. Here, in August 1969, Olympian 1208 makes its way along the Ogwr valley towards Ogmore by Sea, passing, on the other side of the river, at Merthyr Mawr, the highest sand dunes in Europe. Following withdrawal in 1971 this bus would see further service with Telford Coachways. *Roger Davies*

▲ The first Tiger Cubs to dual-purpose standard came in 1956. Their 41-seat Willowbrook bodies were fitted with luggage boots for use on express services to Aberystwyth. Delivered in all-over red, they soon gained the new DP livery, which improved their looks. Although officially the renumbering to segregate Leylands from AECs was dated January 1963, the process took more than two years, 481, seen here in Cardiff, becoming 1481 in September 1963. *Chris Taylor collection*

◂ Making Cardiff bus station sound like a racing circuit, the batch of Regent Vs numbered 657-64 had big (9.6-litre) engines and straight-through exhausts. They had lowbridge bodies by Park Royal and were new in March 1956. These were the first ordinary buses to have platform doors — a feature adopted as standard from this time. No 660 is about to roar off on the 26-mile run to Porthcawl via Bridgend. *Chris Taylor collection*

11. Back to Buses

After all the excitement of 1954 but one vehicle joined the fleet in 1955, this being the aforementioned Cridlands chassis — an AEC Regal IV — fitted with the same Willowbrook body as the 1953 delivery. By contrast 1956 saw no fewer than 125 new vehicles enter service, the highest number ever. Among these were 50 more Weymann-bodied Tiger Cubs, while the solitary Olympian had obviously had made its mark, as 40 identical-looking machines of this type came along too, being only slightly heavier than the Tiger Cubs. Also delivered were the company's first dual-purpose Tiger Cubs, 12 of them, with Willowbrook bodywork. And there was a return to double-deckers, 23 of AEC's latest Regent V type, 15 with lightweight chassis and highbridge bodywork, and all with platform doors, a feature that would be standard from now on. Added to all this were the 44 buses from Green's and 21 coaches from Forse — a bumper crop if ever there was one! At the year end the fleet total stood at 732, its highest level ever.

In 1957 there was again but one new bus. No 680, a 73-seat 30ft-long Regent V, made its debut at the 1956 Commercial Motor Show, dwarfing a London Transport Routemaster, not yet in service and in at a tiny 64 seats. It was to be five years before LT caught up with Western Welsh!

We have to go back a bit. With the Green's business Western Welsh acquired its first examples of AEC's lightweight single-decker, the Reliance — four of them, with very tidy Park Royal bodywork. They must have made a favourable impression, as in 1958 18 were introduced into the coach fleet, for which the type would be favoured almost exclusively for nearly 10 years. Giving added élan, the first six were 34-seaters for extended tours and were known collectively as the 'Ambassador' class, the remainder 39-seaters called the 'Capital' class. Nice — and a hint of the old GWR! Experiments with the ex-Green's Reliances had also resulted in the adoption of a most attractive red and ivory livery for dual-purpose vehicles, and the first new examples so painted were the final Leyland Olympians — six, with neat Weymann bodywork featuring, for the first time, three-track route-number blinds; hitherto the company had managed without route numbers, but in January 1958 it was decided to display them.

▲ The highbridge Regents (665-79) that followed in May 1956 shared the same acoustics despite having smaller engines. The whole nature of Barry Island is captured in this delightful shot as 675, in all-over red with the final style of fleetname, sweeps through on a local service. *Chris Taylor collection*

Each area had its own code that made up the first part of the number: 10 was Barry, 14 Brecon, 20 Bridgend, 30 Cardiff, 40 Carmarthen, 50 Crosskeys, 60 Neath, 70 Pontypool and 80 Haverfordwest. They also used yellow numbers, something with which Western Welsh was way ahead of the game. In a nice twist, the last Olympian, 490, appeared at the 1958 Show.

By now the company's deteriorating financial position had forced it to look again at double-deckers. For years manufacturers had been trying to resolve the low-bridge problem, and AEC, in conjunction with Park Royal, had come up with the aptly named Bridgemaster. Western Welsh took 20 in 1959, and the first, 683, joined 490 at the 1958 Show — which just goes to show the prestige the company had. There were also 30 more Tiger Cubs, six being dual-purpose vehicles. The remaining 24 were the first buses to be delivered fully equipped for one-man operation. Older members of the fleet started to follow suit.

We may as well carry on to the end with this subject. In vehicular terms 1960 was a year of extremes. Leyland had come up with its revolutionary Atlantean, with rear engine, front entrance and almost flat floor, with all the design complexities

The 40 Leyland Olympian/Weymann saloons of 1956 were virtually indistinguishable from contemporary Tiger Cubs. Still in original livery, 1239 is seen amongst other buses in all-over red at Brecon in August 1964. Tiger Cub 1166 next to it has the simplified and less impressive crest on its front panel — a good comparison with that on 1239, whose advert shows an old connection with the Hancocks Brewery. Two of those, please! *Geoff Gould* ▸

In 1957 only one bus entered service — but what a bus! No 680 was a huge, 73-seat AEC Regent V to the newly permitted 30ft length. It boasted a convertible open-top body as seen here at the bodybuilders, Park Royal, but is never known to have operated as such. It had a fully automatic gearbox which turned out to be problematic, so this was soon changed for a semi-automatic. It cost £5,445 new. *Viv Corbin collection* ▾

▴ Four Park Royal-bodied AEC Reliances were among the 44 vehicles acquired in December 1956 with Green's Motors of Haverfordwest and numbered 597-600 (later 267-70) with WW. The first two were to dual-purpose specification and were experimentally repainted wine red with ivory roof. This led to the adoption of this livery for DPs — and the purchase of further Reliances. No 597 is seen in Cardiff bus station. *Viv Corbin collection*

◂ The first AEC Reliance coach, 101, is posed here at Llandaff Cathedral, a favourite location for official WW shots. The six Harrington-bodied coaches forming the 'Ambassador' class had 34 seats and were new for the 1958 touring season. After eight years with WW, No 101 was to see further service with an operator in Yorkshire. *Viv Corbin collection*

◂ The final Olympians, delivered in 1958, had Weymann dual-purpose bodywork and wore the attractive DP livery of the day. They were the first vehicles in the fleet to have route-number blinds. Here 487 (later 1487) is followed by an earlier, bus-bodied Olympian at Ebbw Vale Crossing (as the timetable would have it) in August 1960. *Tony Warrener*

▲
In 1959, 24 Tiger Cubs became the first WW buses to be delivered fully equipped for one-man operation, although 1240 here in Cardiff is conductor-operated, as the pay-as-you-enter sign on the nearside front is covered by a flap. BET designs were taking a turn for the worse, and these Park Royal bodies lacked the style of previous types. At least it is livened up by the cream (almost yellow) band, one of which remains. *Chris Taylor collection*

▲ Between them Park Royal and AEC could make Bridgemasters look frightful, but the 20 received by Western Welsh in 1959 were rather sleek and attractive things. No 698 shows off its all-over red livery at Haverfordwest in July 1970. (Note how all its manufacturer's badging has been removed!) With the Eastern Valleys co-ordination scheme there was an increase in the requirement for Western Welsh low-height double-deckers (Pontypool having traditionally been an all-saloon depot), but the engineers wanted more modern types, preferring the Bridgemasters to go west for an easier life. This restricted the options for one-man operation in West Wales and in its way was a further contributory factor to the problems in that area. *Kenneth Evans*

◄ The first Atlanteans arrived in time to sport the cream/yellow stripes. Alan Roberts remembers his first sight of one: 'My whole world was being turned upside down; where would it all end? There was talk of not knowing whether they were coming or going.' Roger Davies was so surprised that he had to rush home and draw one, cameras not being commonplace. No 304 was one of the first 12, all of which were sold, following a holiday conversation with former WW man Lyndon Rees, to China Motor Bus in Hong Kong. WW painted them up in CMB's then orange and cream livery before export. An old wag at Ely Works looked at one and remarked: 'Funny — the buggers boiled going to Barry Island!' No 304 became PDR7 in the CMB fleet. *Chris Taylor collection*

that entailed; as supplied to Western Welsh, with semi-lowbridge Weymann bodywork seating 70, it also solved most of the interior problems of the earlier lowbridge types. It seemed like the answer to Western Welsh's dreams, and 31 came along. At the other end of the scale, the Albion Nimbus, a cheap and cheerful 30-seater, seemed the answer to the rural bus problem, and 24 joined the fleet. Jumping ahead, 24 more Nimbus came in 1961 and 35 more Atlanteans in 1962. A bit of a disaster, then, that both types proved seriously unreliable. Chris Taylor remembers the Nimbuses as the only diesel buses he ever heard backfiring! After much work with Leyland, not to say expense, Western Welsh could finally claim reasonable reliability from the Atlanteans. Most of the Nimbuses were to remain in the fleet for only five or six years, but in any case, the services for which they were intended were having a pretty torrid time.

Back in 1960 six more Reliance coaches arrived, forming the 'Cambrian' class of 36-seaters for tour work, this time with a design of body concocted between Weymann and Western Welsh and not to be found elsewhere. The dual-purpose requirement was met by 12 Tiger Cubs. An unusual move was the purchase of second-hand buses for work on a contract at an oil refinery in Milford Haven. This required single-deckers and low-height double-deckers, so some of the second-hand buses, being highbridge, were allocated to Cardiff, Barry and Bridgend to release lowbridge types.

In 1961 the 'Cambrian' class was augmented by six more Reliances, whilst nine more 39-seaters formed the 'Celtic' class, a description chosen from 66 entries in a 'name a coach' competition. Mr Albert Higgins of Cardiff received a prize of one guinea (£1.05) for his suggestion, which thankfully was chosen in preference to 'Meteor', 'Carmillion' and 'Gaudeamus'. Phew! But this year the dual-purpose requirement was met by Reliances too, 12 of them. There was also a Ford minibus, which, although licensed as a bus, was used solely for staff transport.

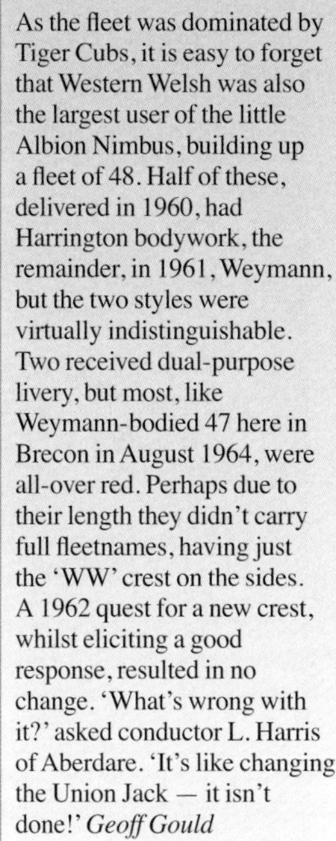

◄ As the fleet was dominated by Tiger Cubs, it is easy to forget that Western Welsh was also the largest user of the little Albion Nimbus, building up a fleet of 48. Half of these, delivered in 1960, had Harrington bodywork, the remainder, in 1961, Weymann, but the two styles were virtually indistinguishable. Two received dual-purpose livery, but most, like Weymann-bodied 47 here in Brecon in August 1964, were all-over red. Perhaps due to their length they didn't carry full fleetnames, having just the 'WW' crest on the sides. A 1962 quest for a new crest, whilst eliciting a good response, resulted in no change. 'What's wrong with it?' asked conductor L. Harris of Aberdare. 'It's like changing the Union Jack — it isn't done!' *Geoff Gould*

◄ Two of the 1960 Harrington-bodied Albion Nimbuses, Nos 2 and 24, were delivered as DPs and wore appropriate livery. They were used on the Rhoose Airport service and were later repainted blue and ivory. No 2 here was also one of two (the other being No 10) to gain a flat windscreen at some stage.
Chris Taylor collection

◄ Unique to WW was this design of Weymann body — a joint project by the two firms and one of the very few British designs to feature truly Continental-style windscreens. The first six, on AEC Reliance chassis, arrived in 1960 and were known collectively as the 'Cambrian' class. This somewhat ghostly picture shows 124 dressed up to go to that year's British Coach Rally at Brighton, where it won a cup. *Chris Taylor collection*

▲ In order to release low-height buses for a contract in Milford Haven WW bought some buses from South Wales and Devon General. The latter were highbridge and operated from Barry, Bridgend and Cardiff. Used for only a few months, they retained their original livery, with fleet numbers slightly modified. Seen in Barry, 1562 (ex DR562) was a Weymann-bodied AEC Regent III new in 1948. *Roger Davies collection*

▲ The very smart DP livery lifted any body style, as is apparent from this view of 1271, a 1960 Weymann-bodied Tiger Cub PSUC1/2, in Bridgend on the Porthcawl–Pontypridd service worked jointly with Rhondda. Stylishly, only the crest was carried on the sides. Note that the company crest is also proudly displayed on the canteen wall. *Chris Taylor collection*

The year 1962 was notable in that it brought the first single-deckers to the newly authorised maximum length of 36ft. These buses, Leyland Leopards with Willowbrook bodywork, seated 54 and once again offered an alternative to the double-decker.

It was with obvious relief that Western Welsh returned to front-engined double-deckers, in the form of 10 attractive Northern Counties-bodied Regent Vs delivered in 1963. These had forward entrances and were praised for their simplicity of design — an indication of the impact of the Atlanteans! They were followed by 21 Leyland PD2s with Weymann bodywork to the same layout. Nine Tiger Cubs also arrived, along with

◄ Two of the 1961 delivery of Willowbrook-bodied Reliances, headed by 280 (or maybe it was still 1280 then), park on Cardiff Bridge, just by the castle, on an Omnibus Society tour. The rather insipid livery, not helped by the apologetic fleetname, didn't last long, and these buses reverted to the normal 'more red' scheme, some even gaining blue and ivory and then red bus livery. Colourful lot! *Arnold Richardson / Photobus*

◄ The company's first 36ft-long saloons came in 1962 in the shape of 18 imposing Willowbrook-bodied Leopards. These were fitted with a wide entrance — 'a noticeable new feature', according to the *Bulletin*. They also had semi-automatic four-speed gearboxes (as in the Atlanteans), but, like many other operators, Western Welsh specified air rather than electric operation for these buses, to overcome driver abuse. They became a familiar sight on the 'low road' — the 304 service linking Barry with Cardiff via Dinas Powys — and on the Bridgend valley routes, particularly the 212 and 222. No 608 is seen doing just that in Maesteg in July 1962. These were the first saloons delivered in all-over red, and, true to form, 602 appeared at the 1962 Show. *Geoff Gould*

After the traumas of the Atlanteans Western Welsh engineers couldn't contain their glee when 10 Regent Vs turned up in 1963. 'Built for easy maintenance, the chassis has standard leaf springs and conventional engine, synchromesh gearbox and transmission layout,' they reported. The batch also introduced forward entrances on front-engined buses, fluorescent lighting and extensive use of plastic materials 'to keep a high standard of cleanliness', and they were very pleasant buses in which to travel. Curiously, after 66 70-seaters, they reverted to a shorter length with only 65 seats in their attractive Northern Counties bodies. Both Rhondda and South Wales did this too, which seems a bit odd; perhaps it was to do with fuel consumption. No 706 in Cardiff also shows off the subtle difference between WW red and Rhondda red, as seen on the bus on the right.
Arnold Richardson / Photobus

The good people at Weymann seemed to 'pinch' the front of double-deckers to ridiculous lengths when bodying 'tin-front' Leylands such as this, but the buses were well liked at Barry. Cardiff-allocated 906, a 1963 delivery, is working to Penarth on a long-established joint service with Cardiff Corporation, one of whose Alexander-bodied AEC Swifts is seen behind. There are some nice N&C coaches in the background too.
Colin Scott

the company's first 36ft coaches — Leyland Leopards with Duple Alpine Continental bodywork of imposing appearance, well set off in early company photographs of one against the dramatic cliffs of Southerndown. Later in the year one was fitted with a cocktail bar and used for a tour of South Wales steelworks by United Nations delegates from 23 countries. It is interesting that the company stuck to Leylands for longer vehicles, not sampling AEC's offerings.

But then it was Tiger Cub time again. Over the next four years no fewer than 106 new ones were delivered, all with the stylish BET-style bodywork, with wrap-around windscreen, supplied by a number of bodybuilders, some being finished to dual-purpose specification. On the coach front there was a return to shorter vehicles and therefore AEC, which in 1964 provided six Reliances with Harrington bodywork; 17 more, with Plaxton's revolutionary Panorama coach body, came in the next three years, along with 15 Marshall-bodied dual-purpose vehicles in 1967. With the move to 36ft coaches there was a change to Leyland Leopards from 1968. From 1965 until 1971 all coaches and dual-purpose vehicles received a delightful ivory and blue livery; the old sentiments had won out at last! Leopards with 36ft bus bodywork augmented the bus fleet (well, you couldn't get a long Tiger Cub!), and finally, in 1971, the company began to take short Leopards, its beloved Tiger Cub having by now ceased production. The same year saw a brief (seven-month) flirtation with the 36ft Bristol RE before all examples moved to South Wales Transport. Double-deck requirements were fulfilled from 1964 by a new AEC product, the Renown, Western Welsh building up a fleet of 28, with magnificent Northern Counties bodywork, until production ceased. From 1969 Atlantean deliveries resumed in small numbers, but unfortunately the low height requirement obliged the company to buy the PDR1/3 model, which was not the most reliable.

From here on this part of our tale becomes entwined with the next, so we'd best move on. Suffice it to say that throughout the turbulent 'Sixties, whatever was going on behind the scenes, the buses were well presented; it still looked like the glory days. The early pioneers would have been proud.

In 1963 four elegant additions were made to the touring fleet. WW's first coaches to the newly permitted 36ft length, they had Duple Alpine Continental bodywork on Leyland Leopard chassis, which seemed to be the company's preference for longer vehicles. The 49 seats were upholstered with an imitation tartan design (for Scottish tours, perhaps?), and there were two heating systems and air-conditioning, provided by blowers fitted above each seat and controlled by passengers. Based at Crosskeys, Neath and Cardiff, these splendid coaches were also available for private hires and day excursions. The Press were impressed too. On 3 May they were given a tour through the narrow lanes of the Vale of Glamorgan, ably piloted by Cardiff driver Bert Angulatta. The *Western Mail* proclaimed it 'superb'. Trouble is ... if you leave one lying around while on a tour the local operator is likely to pinch it for express work — just as Ribble has done here with 143, seen entering Rawtenstall on its way to Wakefield! Delivered in overall ivory, it had by now gained the blue livery, which clashed slightly with the red trim. *Roger Davies collection*

▲ The 1964 delivery of Tiger Cubs carried Willowbrook bodies to the new and much improved BET style with wraparound screens. Nos 1328-33 were delivered in a revised dual-purpose livery (the normal one is on the bus alongside) but no other concessions were made — they were basically 45-seat buses. They did have luggage boots though — shades of the old WW! They didn't last long like this, being painted into bus livery the following year at the same time as blue-and-cream was chosen for coaches and DPs. *Chris Taylor collection*

In full tour guise, complete with 'dustbin lids', 1966 Reliance/Plaxton 157 stands outside Cardiff bus station. In the background is the Empire Pool, built for the 1958 Commonwealth Games and since swept away to make room for the Millennium Stadium.
Arnold Richardson / Photobus

Interior of No 153, one of the six AEC Reliance coaches with 36-seat Plaxton Panorama bodywork purchased for the 1965 season. Note the flamboyant representation of the WW motif on the antimacassars. Curtains were then becoming the norm on new coaches.
Viv Corbin collection

The last 20 Tiger Cubs, with Marshall bodies, came in 1967. Outwardly similar to the others, 1399 was in fact very different, being fitted with a Voith automatic gearbox and retarder. The gearbox eliminated the need for a clutch, and was therefore two-pedal controlled. The company intended it to reduce wear and tear on vehicles owing to 'ever-increasing traffic congestion and the tendency to speed up schedules'. Keeping alive a WW tradition of attendance, it was used as a demonstrator by Voith at the 1967 Commercial Motor Show at Earl's Court, where it is seen complete with white Cwmbran allocation diamond. The Daimler Roadliner next to it was briefly used by Neath & Cardiff. *Chris Taylor collection*

In the company of a Reliance/Harrington coach, two brand-new Leopards with 51-seat bodywork by Marshall prepare for work in this busy scene at Neath railway station in July 1969. *Tony Warrener*

At last, in 1971, WW moved on to short Leopards with 45-seat Willowbrook bodies. This photograph reveals that they originally they carried WW fleet numbers in the 5xx series before being renumbered into the 15xx series (to avoid clashing with Rhondda double-deckers). Sister 512 at least managed a run to Porthcawl with its original number. Note also how Rhondda's thin fleet-number style has replaced WW's distinctive chunky style. No 1511, as it became, suffered serious damage on the route it is dressed up for here and became an early repaint into NBC poppy red. *Viv Corbin collection*

Caerphilly Castle is reputedly the second-largest in the UK by area and also used to grace the sides of the local council's buses. It's to the left here as 629, one of the Marshall-bodied Leopards of 1969, climbs up towards the bus station on the lengthy Newport–Merthyr Tydfil route. Moving the fleetname has allowed advertising to be placed on the side panels.
Arnold Richardson / Photobus

Twenty Marshall-bodied Bristol REs were ordered for 1971. The last 15, although registered as UKG 806-20J, did not enter service with Western Welsh, moving directly to South Wales. The first five lasted barely seven months before moving to South Wales in January 1972. So this picture in Cardiff of 803 working a 303 to Tredegar in December 1971 is a bit of a rarity. It carries a grey Crosskeys/Cwmbran allocation diamond.
Mike Street

▲ The entire 1965 delivery of Renowns went to St David's, where all three of them, 728-30, are seen in July 1969. They are parked opposite the depot, next to the City Arms Hotel. Note how there are, by now, three different types of radiator trim! Nos 728/9 later moved to South Wales with the Neath-area operations. Fine-looking buses. *Tony Warrener*

◄ The 1971 order for double-deckers called for 10 Alexander-bodied Atlanteans, again the low-height PDR1/3 model. The first five arrived in June and received 'J' registrations. The second five, being due after the change of registration letter in August, were to receive 'K' registrations; indeed, four did but were diverted to East Yorkshire and re-registered in Hull (the fifth, 386, being delivered direct), and voided registration plate VUH 385K graced a workbench at Ely for many years. The first five didn't last long either, being transferred in 1972 to Western National. With orange allocation diamond clearly displayed, 378 is seen in August 1971, working Cardiff crews' least-favourite service. *Tony Warrener*

12. Glory Days Going

Tree-lopping was a necessary 'branch' of the company's activities. This Brush-bodied Regent III (formerly bus 626) of 1948 was converted for these duties in 1961. Seven years later it was sold for scrap for £55. 'Oh no!' we hear the preservationists cry. *Viv Corbin collection*

The 1960s got off to a good start with General Manager T. G. Davies being awarded the OBE. Sadly his health was not too good, and he retired at the end of 1961. A welcome return to the company in 1960 was Ken Allender, who, after a time at Greenslades in Devon, came to oversee the growing coach-tours business. Innovations continued, and in 1961 day trips were offered with picnics, as 'many people find meals in restaurants or hotels too expensive'.

In January 1960 £3,500 was paid to Rhondda Transport for a depot in Treorchy, which seems a little odd. It was; by December 1962 it was to be sold 'at the best possible price'. The weather gave Bridgend another hard time, floods in November 1960 damaging 40 buses. In January 1961 Jack Fox of Barry became the company's first 50-year man. "I haven't regretted a minute of it, the industry has been good to me," he said at the annual long-service-awards dinner. "These 'old sweats' are worth their weight in gold," said the GM. Another Jack was in the news, the Jack Report into the decline of rural bus services, but as soon as it was published it was rubbished as 'unworkable'. Western Welsh was dogmatic: the only solution was the reduction or abolition of fuel tax for buses. It quoted bus route 205 between St Athan and Cowbridge, which earned but one shilling (5p) a mile — half the cost of operation, even with a Nimbus. Fat chance. How differently things might have panned out had governments heeded these calls. They are as much responsible as anything for the decline in bus use.

Still investment took place in property. New offices and a canteen were opened in Bridgend in April 1961, and on Monday 27 November a new bus station and garage was opened in Milford Haven. The Chairman, Mr E. L. Taylor, travelled from London to do the honours; bet he made a weekend of it. The building cost £28,950 and could house nine buses, with parking for a further 17 on open ground, although the allocation rarely exceeded a dozen. There were 28 employees on site, but it was destined for a short life.

January 1962 brought a familiar face when Ivor Gray was appointed General Manager after a stint at Rhondda. He tried his best to build up a rapport between the two companies. Amazing though it seems today, his early days were marred by the immediate and long-term effects of a smallpox epidemic in South Wales.

Driver D. W. Thomas of Bridgend gingerly eases Tiger Cub 1133 through Penprisk during the severe winter of 1962/3. *Viv Corbin collection*

At around this same time Fred Pengelly was on TV talking about rural services and stating that in the whole of Pembrokeshire, Carmarthenshire, Cardiganshire and Breconshire there was only one group of routes that paid its way — those between Haverfordwest and Milford Haven. That was an awful lot of the company under threat. He dismissed the idea of using minibuses, saying that this had been fully investigated and that the costs involved did not justify it. So a 30-seat Nimbus wasn't a minibus. This message continued to be put across, as was the impact of fuel tax, at regular press briefings that took place annually. At these key members of the local press met senior officers, were taken for a spin in the newest coaches, had the coming season's tour programme explained, were told of the company's situation and were invited to ask questions. It was a very far-sighted move.

In March 1962 the old Streamways garage in Penarth was sold, for £9,000, but attempts to sell the Forse garage were still floundering over covenants. However, £60,000 was spent on Ely Works, including a new coach shed. This had the unusual effect of drivers reporting there rather than their home depot during the main coaching season to collect their vehicles.

During 1963 a further £35,000 was spent on new offices at Ely, but some surplus land was sold for housing for £31,000; this brought to an end the exciting adventures of bus enthusiasts prowling through 'The Field', which was full of interesting withdrawn buses. A new 39-bus garage in the new town of Cwmbran was opened in October 1963. It cost £76,664, and the company was later to admit that it had run the local services at a loss for four years until the town became established. Cross-subsidy much closer to home!

Western Welsh often helped out other BET companies, notably City Of Oxford, which company had dreadful problems

Brochures for the opening of Milford Haven depot. Any excuse for another turkey dinner! *Viv Corbin collection*

A 1962 timetable featuring members of the fleet, including a DP Nimbus. *Viv Corbin collection*

▲ As the Thos White operation grew it was decided that a depot and head office was required in Cardiff near the bus termini and railway station. An ideal site was found in Penarth Road — curiously, near Hancocks in Crawshay Street! After planning permission was granted it was decided to use direct labour, so drivers, conductors and fitters all helped with the building. Normal reinforcement was deemed insufficient, so bus chassis, road springs, axles, wheels and ships' wire hawsers by the load were placed in the concrete walls. It passed with the company to WW and is pictured in the mid-1960s, after successive extensions had allowed it to accommodate 30 buses under cover and a further 50 in the parking area behind. Roger Davies got his first proper job in the industry here. It closed in March 1981, was demolished in 2000 and is nowadays the site of a 'Big Yellow' storage depository. *Peter Smith collection*

HOW WE SPEND THE PASSENGERS £

WAGES and SALARIES	13/3¾
MAINTENANCE OF ROLLING STOCK, BUILDINGS, MACHINERY, LUBRICANTS, UNIFORMS, etc.	1/9¼
FUEL	7D
FUEL TAX	1/9¾
NATIONAL & LOCAL TAXES & RATES	3¾D
DEPRECIATION, PROVISION FOR RENEWALS etc.	1/9
DIVIDEND	5½D

◄ 'How we spend the passengers' £', 1963.

[illegible] ROLLING STOCK 1st NOVEMBER 1962

	Co.	S/C.	PAYE S/C.	S/D.	PAYE S/D.	D/D.	TOT.	
CDF	7	10	4	3	5	30	59	2 20 24 25 26 128 130 131 132 133 138 301 316 317 318 319 320 321 336 337 338 339 364 365 496 504 505 539 554 597 598 600 618 633 639 648 664 665 666 667 668 669 670 671 672 680 691 693 701 702 1240 1241 1278 1279 1280 1281 1282 1283 1284
BARRY	3	-	2	12	12	29	58 599	27 28 107 112 155 322 323 324 325 326 340 341 342 343 354 540 610 611 612 613 614 638 643 645 646 655 656 657 673 674 675 676 677 678 679 683 686 [illegible] 1092 1153 1154 1157 1158 1200 1202 1248 1276 1277
X'KEYS	2	5	-	27	2	28	64	23 29 136 302 303 306 307 327 328 329 330 331 344 345 346 347 349 350 351 352 462 494 500 518 541 545 549 661 662 663 684 687 689 697 698 699 962 970 1114 1116 1117 1118 1121 1123 1124 1126 1128 1159 1160 1161 1162 1167 1168 1169 1171 1177 1178 1180 1206 1229 1230 1285 1286 1287
BRECON	1	-	2	-	15	-	18	14 15 16 17 30 115 442 472 489 1051 1052 1089 1102 1164 1165 1166 1176 1261
B'END	1	4	1	64	20	16	106	31 32 33 34 35 36 313 314 315 332 333 334 335 357 358 361 414 415 416 417 418 419 420 421 422 423 424 425 426 428 429 430 431 432 433 434 435 471 480 506 509 520 547 550 551 555 558 559 601 602 603 604 605 606 607 608 609 615 616 617 650 658 659 660 695 700 1017 1018 1019 1023 1024 1025 1027 1032 1055 1056 1074 1084 1087 1088 1095 1097 1103 1112 1115 1131 1132 1133 1134 1135 1141 1143 1144 1145 1207 1212 1220 1221 1228 1231 1232 1249 1250 1251 1270 1271
P'POOL	2	5	-	58	24	-	89	3 4 18 19 21 22 47 108 111 404 405 406 407 408 409 410 411 412 413 427 436 437 438 445 446 453 454 455 456 457 458 459 460 461 469 488 502 503 556 557 1004 1011 1014 1015 1016 1028 1037 1040 1042 1043 1045 1046 1048 1049 1053 1054 1058 1059 1067 1100 1130 1138 1139 1140 1150 1151 1152 1155 1156 1163 1201 1204 1211 1213 1215 1217 1218 1219 1222 1235 1236 1242 1243 1244 1245 1246 1247 1266 1267
P'TALBOT	-	-	-	16	4	-	20	470 542 543 544 548 1007 1008 1012 1013 1020 1022 1065 1071 1072 1101 1108 1109 1111 1214 1224
NEATH	2	7	4	8	7	6	34	37 113 139 304 310 311 312 479 481 482 483 490 491 492 493 495 969 973 1005 1033 1035 1041 1073 1075 1076 1079 1080 1098 1106 1174 1237 1238 1272 1273
A'FORD	-	-	-	2	9	4	15	38 39 305 950 951 954 1036 1078 1093 1104 1105 1142 1227 1254 1255
A'DARE	-	-	1	3	14	4	22	40 308 309 439 440 441 467 468 478 947 972 1006 1063 1064 1066 1077 1110 1120 1125 1137 1252 1253
C'THEN	2	1	-	6	20	2	31	1 8 9 41 42 43 117 448 450 452 463 464 466 522 955 982 1060 1069 1081 1096 1127 1208 1209 1210 1223 1234 1239 1262 1263 1269 1274
N.C.E.	-	-	-	3	4	1	8	447 449 975 1003 1031 1062 1083 1147
N'QUAY	-	-	-	2	4	-	6	13 444 1082 1113 1146 1226
H'WEST	3	4	2	6	13	19	47	5 6 46 110 118 451 474 476 507 508 521 640 649 685 692 694 940 948 949 956 957 960 961 963 968 971 977 978 992 993 1001 1002 1010 1026 1030 1034 1172 1173 1175 1179 1233 1256 1257 1258 1259 1264 1265
M'HAVEN	-	1	1	-	3	5	10	44 45 473 484 653 941 942 943 952 1170
F'GUARD	-	-	-	-	4	-	4	12 1050 1090 1149
ST.DAV	-	2	-	2	5	3	12	7 10 11 443 465 485 546 974 976 979 1205 1275
LIC.	23	39	17	212	165	147	603	
DEL.	29	6	2	13	9	15	74	48 101 102 103 104 105 106 109 114 116 119 120 121 122 123 124 125 126 127 129 134 137 475 477 486 487 501 510 511 512 513 514 515 516 517 519 523 552 553 635 636 637 641 644 651 652 944 945 946 953 958 965 966 967 1039 1044 1047 1057 1061 1085 1086 1094 1099 1107 1119 1122 1129 1136 1148 1203 1216 1225 1260 1268
TOTAL	52	45	19	225	174	162	677	

► Rolling-stock allocation sheet, November 1962. *Stuart Davies collection*

recruiting engineering staff, and whose buses were regular visitors to Ely Works. However, a most interesting development occurred in 1964 whereby a 14-year-old AEC Regent III (coincidentally No 14!) of Cardiff Corporation (which had had 46 buses taken off the road for maintenance reasons) was taken into the works and thoroughly refurbished. This served to demonstrate what the company could do, and all manner of possibilities were raised with regard to expanding its operations in the city. Ultimately these came to naught, but had the company been able to strengthen its position in Cardiff then its fate might well have been very different.

In August 1963, in conjunction with Crosville Motor Services of Chester, Western Welsh had bought Mid Wales Motorways' Newtown–Cardiff service, and this led to the establishment in July 1964 of a Cardiff– Liverpool service. The first service to link North and South Wales, it offered a myriad of onward connections. WW's contribution comprised two AEC Reliances painted ivory and blue, which livery the company liked so much that it decided to treat its entire coach fleet. Sadly a major link with the past was severed when Albert Gray died in August 1964 at the age of 85.

Two events late in 1964 were the withdrawal of service 613 between Carmarthen and Ammanford and the surrender of part of the Carmarthen–Pendine service (410) to Pioneer of Laugharne. In their small way these represented the start of a slippery slope. However, there was doubtless great relief when, in November, the Forse site at Blackweir was finally sold, to the local Kardov flour company for £65,000.

In August 1965 Head Office staff moved back to the extended Ely site after an eight-year sojourn at the bus station in Cardiff. All in all, the recent improvements to the complex at Ely had cost a total of £105,119.

▲ AEC Regent V No 678 pauses in the centre of Penarth. Happily this bus was found, 30 years after withdrawal, in the south of France and has been returned to the UK to regain its former glory. *Peter Smith collection*

▲ The new Cwmbran depot was opened in October 1963. Built to exacting standards at a cost of £76,664, it offered staff excellent facilities. WW's eastern area, consisting of this depot, Crosskeys and Pontnewynydd, had 160 buses at the time, but following the 1967 scheme and the closure of Pontnewynydd this would drop to 120, 65 of them being based at Cwmbran. *Viv Corbin collection*

Further Reliance/Weymann coaches were delivered in 1961, and No 137 was one of nine that made up the 'Celtic' class. Slight modifications were made, including the straightening of the headlights. It is on the Cardiff–Liverpool service, for which it and 134 were painted blue, leading to the adoption of this livery for coaches and DPs. *Chris Taylor collection* ▶

The eight-acre Central Works site at Ely, Cardiff, opened in 1931, and by 1965 a further £140,000 had been spent on extensions to the works and offices. The first picture shows the panel shop where at the time there were 40 coachbuilders, panel-beaters, trimmers and painters out of a total of 190 employed in the works and a further 60 in the Head Office. The second dates from 1960 and shows Leyland Olympic 411 (showing off the rear emergency door of its Weymann body), Tiger Cubs, a PD2 and, on the extreme left, ex-Streamways 537 (LTX 413), a full-fronted Plaxton-bodied Regal III. *Both Viv Corbin collection*

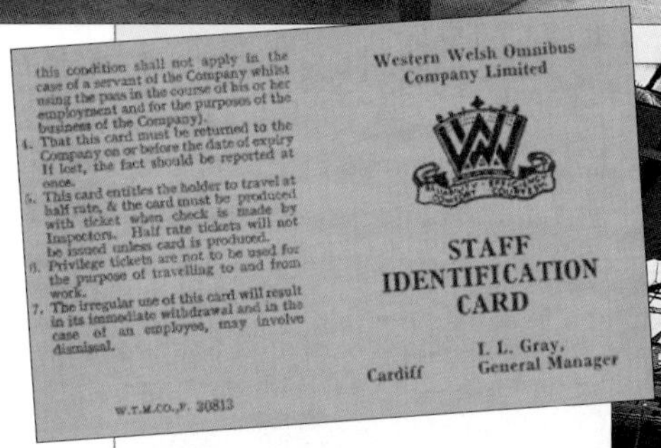

this condition shall not apply in the case of a servant of the Company whilst using the pass in the course of his or her employment and for the purposes of the business of the Company).

4. That this card must be returned to the Company on or before the date of expiry If lost, the fact should be reported at once.
5. This card entitles the holder to travel at half rate, & the card must be produced with ticket when check is made by Inspectors. Half rate tickets will not be issued unless card is produced.
6. Privilege tickets are not to be used for the purpose of travelling to and from work.
7. The irregular use of this card will result in its immediate withdrawal and in the case of an employee, may involve dismissal.

W.T.M.CO.,P. 30813

Western Welsh Omnibus Company Limited

STAFF IDENTIFICATION CARD

Cardiff

I. L. Gray, General Manager

A staff pass from 1967.
Viv Corbin collection

The year 1966 began with the appointment as Chief Engineer of David Cherry, who had previously held that post at Rhondda. This emphasised the closer ties between the two companies, and in June it was announced that they would henceforth be jointly managed. Ivor Gray continued his charm offensive, stating that 'my four years at Rhondda were particularly happy ones'. He went on to assure staff that 'the arrangement does not amount to what has commonly become known as a takeover' and that 'Rhondda will retain its individual identity'.

Ammanford depot was closed in March, most of its services being transferred to South Wales Transport or West Wales Motors. Mr Gray advised that it had been uneconomic for many years.

On 19 July 1966 Mr A. F. R. Carling gave the Chairman's address to the 46th Annual General Meeting of the Western Welsh Omnibus Co. Summarised here, it makes appalling reading. Although a reduced dividend had been paid, the Government had changed the tax laws, so the company paid £17,100 more tax on a smaller dividend. There had been a report — the Wilson Report — into wages and conditions, and its immediate effect was the 1965 wage award, which had cost an extra £140,000. On top of that was the introduction of a sick-pay scheme and a reduction of the working week from 42 to 40 hours without loss of pay. These requirements added another £144,000 to the bill. If that were not enough, revenue at £3,188,500 was £120,000 below estimates, partly due to bad weather. The company had applied to increase fares in May 1965 to take account of the extra costs. The Commissioners waited six weeks before hearing the application, took another month to come up with a decision and then only granted it in part. Appeals were lodged with the Ministry of Transport against the increase by some local authorities and against the reduction in the application by the company. No decision had emerged from Government by the time of the meeting, 14 months after the application. It finally came on 21 July, the day after Prime Minister Harold Wilson had announced a price freeze; not surprisingly, the company's appeal was refused.

A year later Mr Carling observed that there had been 'a refusal to work the machinery of fares control with reasonable promptitude when the result would be politically inconvenient', adding that Western Welsh had been treated unjustly, others having had increases granted before the price freeze. He acknowledged, ruefully, that higher fares were always unpopular; 'perhaps they are more emotive in South Wales than in other places'. This is just to get you in the mood for what comes next.

As a direct result of all this, Port Talbot depot and its outstation at Kenfig Hill closed on 2 October 1966. Port Talbot depot, under the supervision of Inspector-in-Charge Randall Stockton, had operated the service up the Glyncorrwg valley, a Baglan town service and two vehicles on the Bridgend service; the Kenfig Hill shed, at The Square, had been responsible for Porthcawl services 229/230/231. Alternative employment at Bridgend and Neath was refused, so there were 50 redundancies. A new river bridge next to Penarth Road depot in Cardiff necessitated £45,000 of alterations in January 1967, which didn't help the general picture.

Drastic measures were needed, and now these were in the industrial heartland. A major scheme in Monmouthshire, rationalising services, co-ordinating timetables and introducing new, limited-stop services and through fares was implemented on 4 June 1967. This was done jointly with state-owned Red & White,

▼ A most unusual arrangement was the hiring out of season of buses to the Christie Tyler furniture company of Bridgend. All seats were removed, and the vehicles were used as mobile furniture showrooms. These were by no means old vehicles, as this 1965 line-up shows. Tiger Cubs 1328-33 had just been repainted red, and 'Celtic'-class Reliances 131/9 and 'Capital' 113/4/7 were still front-line coaches. All 11 are seen outside the Bridgend factory. *Viv Corbin collection*

A case of 'Guess where this is!'. Heading west out of Cardiff, Park Royal DP-bodied Tiger Cub 1338 of 1965 climbs up The Tumble against a backdrop unrecognisable today. *Viv Corbin collection*

Inspector Edward (Ned) Allsop checks the 306 service between cups of tea in the Pandora Café in Penarth town centre. Who can blame him for taking shelter on this wet and grim day? Ned had 46 years' service with the company when he retired in 1971. In 1963, when steamed-up Regent V/ Northern Counties 707 was new, the fare from Cardiff to Lower Penarth was 1s 3d (6p). *Viv Corbin collection*

which is highly significant. It was the result of two years' work looking at a network of 11 million miles operated by 330 vehicles and 1,000 staff and which had remained largely unchanged since the pioneering days of Eastern Valleys and Western Valleys and the firms of Griffin, Ralph's and Red & White. As part of the agreement (which was formally dated 26 October) Western Welsh closed its depot at Pontnewynydd, near Pontypool, most staff moving to the new centre of operations in Cwmbran, and altogether 33 Western Welsh and 25 R&W buses were saved. Mr Gray advised that 'there is sound logic in these moves; they are in line with the views expressed on behalf of the local authorities and the Minister of Transport, who has called for voluntary co-ordination measures of this kind, but most of all they are necessary if the company is to survive in these highly competitive times.' He did not hide the fact that there would be redundancies, but assured staff that 'we shall not be unmindful of the human problems involved'. As there were no drastic cuts in service frequency, one is forced to the conclusion that it was all long overdue.

One victim of the pooling arrangement was the abolition of time-recording clocks which, owing to the number of operators, had been quite common. Two, however, survived on the 240/244 Pontypridd–Porthcawl routes worked jointly with Rhondda. These were at Church Village and Tonteg, as over this section there were extra buses, co-ordinated with the 240/244, provided by Amalgamated Bus Services, made up of Messrs Bebb, Edwards and Maisey. In the absence of a pooling arrangement the purpose of the clocks was to ensure that there was no 'unfair poaching'. As each bus passed the timing-point the conductor inserted a key into the clock, which registered the time. The recording tapes were analysed weekly, and fines imposed — 2 shillings (10p) per minute up to 5 minutes late and 10 shillings (50p) over 5 minutes late; there was no fine for early running. At a time when the single fare over this section was 7d (3p) and the fare for the full length of the route only 4s 9d (24p) this was serious stuff!

The political regime had made it quite clear that, one way or another, it was going to nationalise BET. Negotiations took place during 1967, a price of £35 million was agreed upon, and BET was bought by the state-owned Transport Holding Company on 13 May 1968. The new, amalgamated group, called the National Bus Company (shades of the old SWCM GWR days!), commenced trading on 1 January 1969. Given all this it is frankly startling that plans proceeded for a new depot costing £70,000 in Haverfordwest.

It is heartening to note that, despite everything, the company still felt willing and able to help local communities. In 1965 an ex-Red & White Tiger was converted with rear wheelchair lift for the Danybryn Cheshire Home, the task, taking 2,120 man hours, being undertaken in free time by Central Works staff. In 1970 a mock-up of the front of a single-decker was built for Rockwood Hospital, which specialised in helping disabled people who had difficulty with everyday tasks, like getting on a bus. Again time and materials were given free by the company and its suppliers, and the finished product received fleet number 1600!

The last six Olympians (485-90), delivered in 1958, had Weymann dual-purpose bodies and were the first buses fitted with number blinds, a fact lost on this driver! In 1967 they were downgraded to buses and repainted accordingly; here 1488 (as it has become) shows the revised crest, all-over red livery and a grey Crosskeys allocation diamond as it enters Bassaleg. *Chris Taylor collection*

For a while the company toyed with the idea of re-using the bodywork fitted to the Albion Nimbuses. Accident-damaged No 27 provided the opportunity to experiment, its body being lifted and fitted to a new Bristol LHS chassis. In common with other members of the fleet it had a Leyland O.400 engine but was now fitted with a Turner Clark five-speed gearbox, a new type to the company; the Bristol chassis was also 8in longer in the wheelbase and had a front-mounted radiator, while the cab was supplied by the manufacturer as a single, draught-proof unit, so there was much modification to be done. The bus duly emerged as No 1 and was used for a trail run at a conference held at Ely on 23 April 1968. Extensive trials followed, but no further conversions took place, and No 1 was usually to be found on the Rhoose Airport service. It may have been small, but it was a monster to drive. *Chris Taylor*

Port Talbot was a notorious traffic bottleneck as a result of a level crossing right in the town centre. At busy times it was quite usual for a passenger to be able to hop out of a car, do some shopping and return, the car having moved only a few feet. It caused havoc to bus schedules. Here, in the summer of 1962, a Tiger Cub DP has passed the hold-up to continue on its way from Ammanford to Cardiff. Several Thomas Bros Tiger Cubs in their smart blue livery wait their turn. The famous steelworks dominates the skyline. *Tony Warrener*

13. A Bit of National Bus

It's April 1970, and Olympian 1226 is pulling out of Glangwili Hospital in Carmarthen on the cross-town route to Johnstown (Cow & Gate Creamery). These services would eventually pass to local operator Dan Jones, ultimately being taken over from Davies Blossom by FirstGroup; the site of the post office (to the left of the bus) is now occupied by First's centre of operations in the area. *Kenneth Evans*

Mr T. W. H. Gailey CBE, Chairman of the National Bus Company, wrote to all his new charges early in 1969: 'I trust that you will feel with me that the formation of NBC will herald a new era in road passenger transport in England and Wales. It provides us with an opportunity to improve upon an efficient and viable industry. Our aim is unchanged: to provide the best possible service to the public in an economical way. I know I can count on your support.' But perhaps not everyone did feel that way.

At Western Welsh little changed at first, but the new order made itself felt in March, when the parcels operation passed to the National Freight Corporation. There were two significant departures, the first being Lyndon Rees. Latterly Assistant to the Traffic Manager, he had been with Western Welsh since 1959 and was well known throughout the company; indeed, he had done a lot of the work on the 1967 co-ordination scheme. He went to Hong Kong, firstly to China Motor Bus before making his name building up the highly successful and well-known Citybus company. Then, in October, Leslie Gray retired after 50 years. He wrote: 'I would express my thanks for the friendly co-operation … which has made the job so satisfying at all times.' His daughter Christine remembers that their life revolved around the company; her mother was one of the first shorthand typists. Her father took her around the company as a small child in his Austin Seven; 'I can still smell those depots.' Their doorbell was taken from a bus, and beside the door was a 'Have you forgotten anything?' notice. 'If it didn't move, my father painted it,' she recalls; 'I still have his hoe painted Western Welsh red.'

Apprentice David Patterson and signwriter Peter Mitchell put the finishing touches to a repaint of Ford Thames 4D parcel van No 19. This was one of five similar vans and trucks in the fleet. The vans were an excellent advertising medium travelling throughout South Wales. PBO 846 was retired in October 1967, some 18 months before the parcels business passed to the National Freight Corporation. *Chris Taylor collection*

In April 1970 the splendid new depot in Haverfordwest opened. It wasn't exactly an indication of what lay ahead in West Wales. For 1970 the company as a whole recorded a loss of £269,565 on

a fleet of 527. (Wonder what the Chairman of BET must have been thinking!) NBC might have so far done little, but it had big plans for its operations in South Wales. 1971 was to be a momentous year.

On 1 January Rhondda was taken over by Western Welsh. Ivor Gray put a brave face on it. 'The name will remain the same yet awhile, but, ultimately, who knows? So let's face the new year together and resolve to do everything we can to help the industry in its present difficulties.' It was never going to work. The fleetname did disappear, as, indeed, did most of the fleet, with indecent haste. The staff never fitted in; Rhondda was a proud company stretching back to 1906 and regarded Western Welsh as an upstart. It was a unique part of a unique community and had its own, shall we say, idiosyncrasies. The appointment of a Cardiff driver as an inspector at Porth brought the threat of a strike and a climbdown. The fleetname came back too. The idea might have looked sensible in NBC's Headquarters in New Street Square, London, but it didn't in Porth Square.

If the Rhondda takeover was a bad idea, the absorption on the same date by South Wales of Neath & Cardiff Luxury Coaches was worse. As part of the deal Western Welsh got the six coaches (and the drivers) allocated to Cardiff. Possibly as a result of pent-up frustration at never having taken it over, the two larger companies soon abolished N&C's hugely popular image, and before long the Swansea–Cardiff service had become just any old bus route. It was a stupid decision.

In the same month St David's and Fishguard depots closed, with 52 redundancies and the loss of 17 routes. The former dated only from 1954, the latter from just 1959. There were further redundancies, 21 at shiny new Haverfordwest and eight at Carmarthen. Fred Pengelly summed it up. 'For years we have operated, at a loss, services in rural areas … subsidised by our more profitable urban services. But the point has been reached where they are being undermined by spiralling costs and a marked decline in the number of passengers.' He went on to

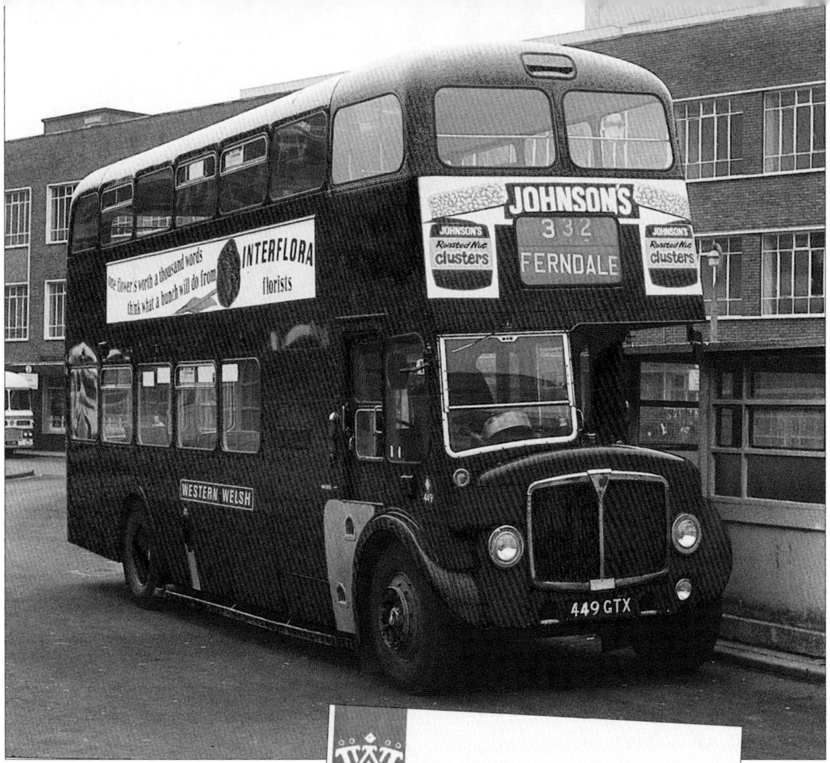

◄ The Rhondda fleet from the late 1950s onwards was characterised by these big, forward-entrance AEC Regent Vs. Curiously, despite being right in the middle of the coalfields, the company never felt the need, unlike Western Welsh, to stick to low-height buses. Following the WW takeover the fleet seemed to be disposed of with indecent haste, many of the Regents, fitted with Gardner engines and Daimler gearboxes, going to Hong Kong. Few gained Western Welsh fleetnames, but 449 here did and was allocated to Cardiff as a part-time trainer, hence the brackets for 'L' plates. In this May 1972 shot in Cardiff it is working the joint 332 service to Maerdy, a familiar haunt in its Rhondda days. At the end of the year it became No 2A2 with Kowloon Motor Bus. *Mike Street*

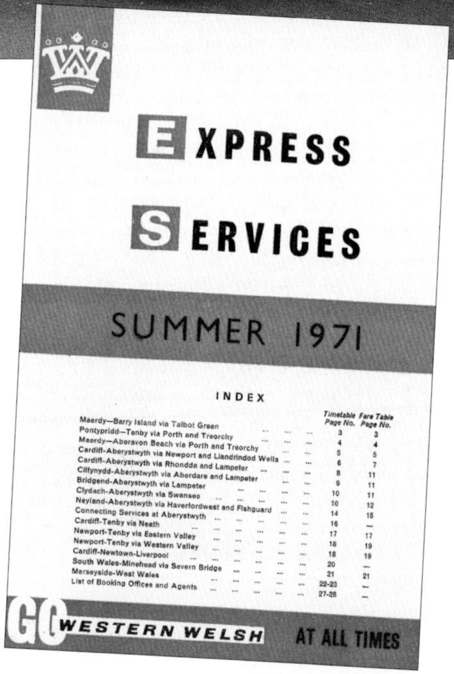

EXPRESS SERVICES

SUMMER 1971

INDEX

	Timetable Page No.	Fare Table Page No.
Maerdy—Barry Island via Talbot Green	3	3
Pontypridd—Tenby via Porth and Treorchy	4	4
Maerdy—Aberavon Beach via Porth and Treorchy	5	5
Cardiff-Aberystwyth via Newport and Llandrindod Wells	6	7
Cardiff-Aberystwyth via Rhondda and Lampeter	8	11
Cilfynydd-Aberystwyth via Aberdare and Lampeter	9	11
Bridgend-Aberystwyth via Lampeter	10	11
Clydach-Aberystwyth via Swansea	10	12
Neyland-Aberystwyth via Haverfordwest and Fishguard	14	15
Connecting Services at Aberystwyth	16	—
Cardiff-Tenby via Neath	17	17
Newport-Tenby via Eastern Valley	18	19
Newport-Tenby via Western Valley	18	19
Cardiff-Newtown-Liverpool	20	—
South Wales-Minehead via Severn Bridge	21	21
Merseyside-West Wales	22-23	—
List of Booking Offices and Agents	27-28	—

GO WESTERN WELSH AT ALL TIMES

◄ Express brochure, 1971.
Stuart Davies collection

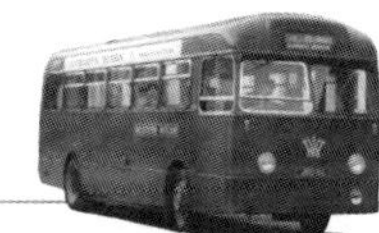

The 1972 Leopard/Marshalls were the first (and, as it turned out, only) DPs to be delivered in the revived livery of wine red and ivory, introduced in that year to replace blue. Motorists' blatant disregard for parking regulations gives the driver of 1522 a hard time as he picks his way through Cowbridge *en route* from Swansea on the old Neath & Cardiff service. Cowbridge had had a dreadful congestion problem until bypassed; the removal of through traffic obviously made the locals feel free to use the roads as they wished! As this is 1973, it is very likely that Roger Davies had allocated this Cardiff driver his turn. *Richard Mellor*

explain that the company could no longer subsidise them, 'but the local authorities could by taking advantage of the 1968 Transport Act, which gives a 50% government subsidy to match any support from rates'. They didn't, but more enlightened councils in Brecon and Cardigan had granted a reprieve to services there.

In April the Gray dynasty at WW ended with the retirement of Ivor Gray. He signed off by saying he would do it all again; 'My warmest thanks to you all for being such a grand bunch.' He was replaced by Keith Holmes from Northern General.

In May Aberdare depot closed with 14 redundancies and the transfer of 23 staff to the Red & White depot just down the road. The WW depot dated from 1939, and the staff were famous for their interest in first-aid activities, competing in numerous national competitions. The same month saw the closure of Carmarthen depot, with the loss of 45 jobs. Fred Pengelly was to the point again, stating that 'the direct cause of this was the refusal of the local authority to co-operate with us by offering a subsidy towards the cost of many thousands of unremunerative miles.' He admitted that the failure of local staff to agree to one-man operation of the town services was a contributory factor, adding that, whilst it wouldn't have saved the depot, it would have reduced job losses. In January 1972 the nine-bus depot at Milford Haven, barely 10 years old, was closed too.

At this point it is perhaps worth pondering the situation in West Wales. It may be that there was more that the company could have done in terms of introducing one-man operation and reviewing services. And it is interesting that in private hands the company had soldiered on but when nationalised it didn't. But one can't help feeling that, having enjoyed investment in facilities and services that had, in effect, been paid for by the people of Glamorganshire and Monmouthshire, the local councils could have paid back a little. It was a rotten way to behave.

NBC's grand plan continued in 1972 with the transfer in January of Neath, its 35 buses and 1957-built depot and in March of Haverfordwest, its 1970-built depot, 70 staff, 11 routes and 22 buses to South Wales Transport, all for £200,000. This might have looked sensible on paper, but the existing arrangement had worked perfectly well for many years, and it is difficult to see the benefits of changing it; in West Wales Swansea was hardly likely to be viewed more favourably than Cardiff. What the staff must have felt and how much it all cost we can only guess at. Alan Roberts well remembers the friendly Neath staff from his youth, one even plucking him and his bicycle off a mountainside in gathering gloom and returning him home. In effect now cut off, Newcastle Emlyn and New Quay, with 11 buses and 20 staff, were transferred in April to Crosville, for £23,693.

▲ St David's Day 1971 is the date of this scene in Haverfordwest as coach 183 waits for an official party that included HRH The Prince of Wales. No 183 was a Plaxton Panorama-bodied Leyland Leopard new in 1970 seating 49 and painted in NBC's short-lived coach livery featuring the company colour (still blue) and a large block fleetname. These fine 36ft-long coaches featured power steering, two-speed axles, exhaust brakes and power-operated doors. *Viv Corbin collection*

▲ Tiger Cub/Weymann 1135 of 1956 tootles about on Carmarthen town services in August 1964. The refusal to agree to one-man operation contributed to these services' demise in 1971, but the blame lay primarily with the local authority. *Geoff Gould*

Limited one-man operation of double-deckers was achieved in West Wales using four 1969 Northern Counties-bodied Atlanteans. No 374 works the service from Haverfordwest to St David's, which, in a throwback to GWR days, still started from the railway station at the former, where the bus is seen in September 1970. Was the hearse symbolic of the fate awaiting Western Welsh services in the area? No 374 would pass to South Wales in 1972, becoming its 902. *Kenneth Evans* ▶

The 1967 delivery of 15 DPs had Marshall bodywork and marked a change of chassis to the AEC Reliance. All 15 passed to South Wales Transport with Neath area operations in 1972 but retained their fleet numbers. No 205 is at Weston-super-Mare on August Bank Holiday Monday 1973 in full pre-NBC South Wales livery. *Mike Street*

A delightful but sad scene inside Carmarthen depot in April 1971 as a conductor makes his way out for another spell of duty — possibly his last, for the depot closed the next month. The bus is 1313, a Willowbrook-bodied Tiger Cub and one of the first (1964) batch with curved-screen BET styling. *Kenneth Evans*

Cardigan in 1973, and Tiger Cub 1344 with Marshall 41-seat DP body from the 1965 batch shares a stand with West Wales 700 BTH, a Yeates-bodied Bedford. Although the Tiger Cub is in full WW livery, the date and the route number give the game away, and by now 1344 is really Crosville STL934. *Richard Mellor*

Some buses transferred to Crosville gained that operator's final pre-NBC style of livery and fleetname and were painted at Ely. Formerly Western Welsh 1353, Crosville STL936, a Park Royal-bodied Tiger Cub of 1965, stands inside Aberystwyth depot in August 1973. *Kenneth Evans*

The first short Leopards of 1971, bodied by Willowbrook, were also the last DPs delivered in the pleasing blue and ivory livery. They started a new fleet-number series, as their intended numbers in the 5xx series had been taken by Rhondda double-deckers. No 1509 is in Berw Road, Pontypridd, in March 1973 on limited-stop service 330 from Ynysybwl to Cardiff. This was created by extending one of the Western Welsh Cardiff–Pontypridd services to cover the Red & White local 183 service to Ynysybwl — a further example of the closer ties between the two companies. It was a bit of a con, however, as the Cardiff service was reduced from a 15-minute frequency to half-hourly with the hourly 330 superimposed, giving an unbalanced frequency. Such were the times. Oh, and you *can* have a word that long apparently without a vowel, as both 'w' and 'y' are vowels in Welsh. *Geoff Gould*

There is a strange quirk of British bus design that many types, having improved to a point of near perfection, promptly get replaced. Such was the case with the Leyland Leopard, and the 24 service saloons delivered to WW in 1972 prove the point. Featuring a higher driving position than previous models and fitted with the beefier O.680 engine, these were magnificent vehicles to drive, while the 51-seat Marshall bodywork incorporated various improvements learned from earlier buses: the front dash and cab were matt black (to cut down glare), a revised colour of Formica was used internally, and they were equipped with a Clayton U28 heating system and demister to 'materially improve standards'. No 1553 is seen here in Cwmbran next to 1528, one of the DP versions. Next came Leyland Nationals …
Colin Scott

◂ Briefly, after the blue and before poppy red, DPs reverted to red and ivory. The fleetname was red-backed for use on all types of vehicle and, whilst standing out, did look a bit odd. No 1345, a 1965 Tiger Cub/Park Royal, pulls out of Llanhilleth in June 1973 on Blackwood–Brynmawr service 120, which formed part of the Monmouthshire and Breconshire co-ordination scheme. This picture just sums up Western Welsh. *Geoff Gould*

If this battering were not enough, Western Welsh gradually came under the influence of Red & White, which by now included Jones of Aberbeeg. In August Keith Holmes became General Manager of both, and upon the departure in October of David Cherry to Northern Counties — an appropriate move — Mr R. O. Blatchford of R&W took over as Chief Engineer of both fleets. Excursion programmes were merged, the two companies taking it in turns to operate them. A very popular Cardiff excursion was 'Welsh Mountains and Porthcawl', but suddenly the company was inundated with complaints — the R&W one was different. It was unnecessary to upset staff and customers in this way. With the retirement of Fred Pengelly in September after 37 years with the company, Western Welsh had lost virtually all its senior figures.

Late in 1972 NBC poppy red replaced the rich red livery of the BET era. 'I expect we'll get used to it,' said one senior figure. We didn't. National Travel was set up, taking most coach operations, and the all-over-white livery was applied to these vehicles. By the end of 1973 the fleet was down to 468, and the adoption in 1974 of the batty and worthless Red & White fleet-numbering system just seemed a symbolic final nail in the coffin.

Western Welsh as we knew and loved it was gone.

Tiger Cub Tailpiece

A crest as mounted on depot walls. *Viv Corbin collection*

The later appearance of a WW Tiger Cub, with improved BET-style body and the final style of fleetname with 'lozenge' on the front. No 1368, with 43-seat Park Royal body of 1966, heads for Newport on the lengthy route from Tredegar. *Chris Taylor collection*

Contrasting with 1368 is 1142, one of the 1956 Weymann-bodied Tiger Cubs, seen in Brecon. *Chris Taylor collection*

Acknowledgements

Sincere thanks are due to Monica Richardson, Christine Davies, Ken Evans, Geoff Gould, Rowena Davies *(Thanks, Mum! — Roger)*, Tony Warrener, the late David Kershaw, Stewart Williams (for the fabulous *Bulletins*), Mike Street, Allan Morse and the whole Welsh bus 'Taffia'; also to Richard Mellor, Colin Scott, Andrew Wiltshire, Stuart Jones, Andrew Braddock, Alan Roberts, Stuart Davies, Stephen Phillips, Alan Jarvis, Peter Smith, all at Ian Allan Publishing, Stephen Barber, Richard Saunders, Alec M. Rees, Norrie Thomas, John Reypert, John Woodward and the late Gerald Truran.

Publications found helpful were The Omnibus Society fleet history (PG7), Ian Allan's *British Bus Fleets No 18* (both editions) and Viv Corbin's *The Rise and Fall of National Welsh*.

You can help keep alive the history of buses in South Wales by supporting the Cardiff Transport Preservation Group, which can be contacted at 10 Ger Nant, Ystrad Mynach, Hengoed, CF82 7FE, or online at www.ctpg.co.uk, or the Cardiff & South Wales Trolleybus Project, at 211 Hillrise, Llanedeyrn, Cardiff, CF23 6UQ, or online at www.cardiff-trolleybus.co.uk.

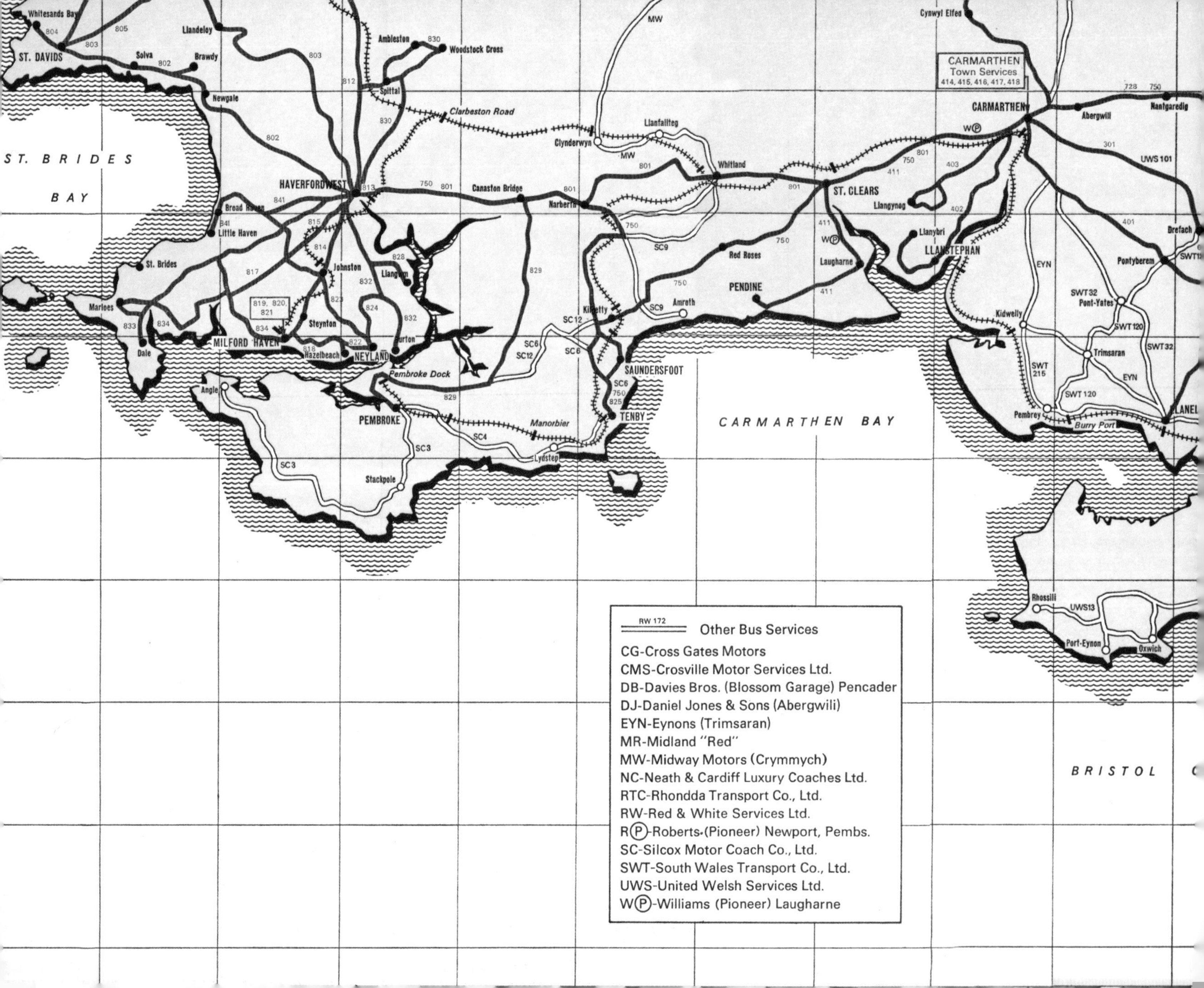

ST. DAVIDS
Whitesands Bay
Solva
Brawdy
Llandeloy
Newgale
Ambleston
Woodstock Cross
Spittal
Clarbeston Road
ST. BRIDES BAY
HAVERFORDWEST
Broad Haven
Little Haven
St. Brides
Marloes
Dale
Johnston
Steynton
MILFORD HAVEN
Hazelbeach
NEYLAND
Llangwm
Burton
Pembroke Dock
Angle
PEMBROKE
Stackpole
Manorbier
Lydstep
TENBY
SAUNDERSFOOT
Kilgetty
Amroth
Canaston Bridge
Narberth
Clynderwyn
Llanfallteg
Whitland
Red Roses
PENDINE
Laugharne
ST. CLEARS
Llangynog
Llanybri
LLANSTEPHAN
Kidwelly
Pembrey
Burry Port
Trimsaran
Pont-Yates
Pontyberem
Drefach
CARMARTHEN
Abergwili
Nantgaredig
Cynwyl Elfed
CARMARTHEN Town Services 414, 415, 416, 417, 418
CARMARTHEN BAY
BRISTOL
Rhossili
Port-Eynon
Oxwich
RW 172
Other Bus Services
CG-Cross Gates Motors
CMS-Crosville Motor Services Ltd.
DB-Davies Bros. (Blossom Garage) Pencader
DJ-Daniel Jones & Sons (Abergwili)
EYN-Eynons (Trimsaran)
MR-Midland "Red"
MW-Midway Motors (Crymmych)
NC-Neath & Cardiff Luxury Coaches Ltd.
RTC-Rhondda Transport Co., Ltd.
RW-Red & White Services Ltd.
R(P)-Roberts (Pioneer) Newport, Pembs.
SC-Silcox Motor Coach Co., Ltd.
SWT-South Wales Transport Co., Ltd.
UWS-United Welsh Services Ltd.
W(P)-Williams (Pioneer) Laugharne